Did God Make Them Black?

Isaac O. Olaleye

TO SOW THE FALLOW SOIL

Winston-Derek Publishers, Inc.
Pennywell Drive—P.O. Box 90883
Nashville, TN 37209

PUBLISHED BY WINSTON-DEREK PUBLISHERS, INC.
Nashville, Tennessee 37205

Library of Congress Catalog Card No: 88-51961
ISBN: 1-55523-223-X

Printed in the United States of America

— DEDICATION —

Dedicated to the human family whose brotherhood transcends the sovereignities of nations,
and who, in true brotherhood, will one day live in
unity like a flock in the pen, and in peace, like
doves in their birdhouse holes.

— Contents —

— PREFACE —

I have no bigoted bones in my body. I am completely neutral to politics, no matter who or what color is involved. All I am trying to do in this book is to examine the seeming physical differences, colors of skin, colors and textures of hair, shapes of nose, intelligence, and equality of people as a whole. And the chief objective of doing so is to help promote better understanding among fellow humans. I sincerely hope that such understanding, which is energetically pursued in this book, will play more than a transient part in making people live together in peaceful harmony regardless of color, language or culture.

ISAAC O. OLALEYE

ONE

SOCIETY AND RACIAL DISCRIMINATION

A seven-year-old girl sat crying on the steps of the First
Baptist Church in Sheepshead Bay, Brooklyn, New York. She was
laboriously scrubbing her arms and legs with cleansing powder,
working desperately to scrub the blackness off her skin. But
instead of rubbing off her pigmentation, her skin became red-
dened and puffy.

Why in the world would a young girl resort to such a drastic
action to change the color of her skin? Because she had been
ridiculed and rejected by her peers who happened to have a skin
color different from hers.

Her eyes were bathed in tears. Tears likewise filled the eyes of
another young woman who grieved: "Black people have been
oppressed so much. Why did God make them black?"

She was a victim of discrimination from which she had no
redress. But did God make her black?

Black South Africans sing: "Oh, God, what have we done? Our
only sin is the color of our skin."

Is their skin black as a result of sin?

It is obvious that the victims of those experiences wished they
could shed their skin color and take up another which would be
acceptable to the society in which they lived. That, of course, is
impossible. So they continue to suffer mental anguish. It is also
highly likely that the seven-year-old's experience had inflicted her
with devastating psychological wounds which may torment her for
the rest of her life. Traumatic experiences encountered in forma-
tive years are usually forever branded in people's minds. How
many young minds in the U.S., Britain and South Africa have

been branded by such indelible emotional scars?

Such touching stories of racial discrimination can be repeated a thousandfold, but we have no interest in flaring up emotions by relating impassioned incidents of racial discrimination, for emotions usually drown out the ability to reason. In such a situation, problems become aggravated instead of alleviated. Clearly, then, the calm, logical and intelligent approach is preferable.

Our main objectives are to show why racial prejudice is practiced, expose the misconceptions people have about the races, relate how racial discrimination affects the oppressed, and above all, show how better understanding of the races can help us all to get along more smoothly with fellow humans.

However, we cannot effectively accomplish our goals without touching on incidents of racial discrimination, and as a result, emotions may be aroused because of the nature of the subject itself. It is difficult to talk about people and their deep-rooted conflicts and yet strip from such a piece of writing any tinge of emotion. Nonetheless, we should try to keep emotions in the background and reasoning in the forefront.

Is the sin of South African blacks and other blacks the color of their skin? How did people feel in the past about black skin?

BLACKS—CURSED BY GOD?

"The black skin of the Negro was not only ugly, but was also the symbol of moral taint and turpitude. (The Negro was the descendant of Ham, and thus accursed, and designed to be of service to his master, the white man." [1])

Other writers, including professed Christians, believed that black people were cursed by God and designed to be slaves. The book *The Race Question in Modern Science* says: "In 1722 the Reverend Thomas Thompson published a monograph, *The Trade in Negro Slaves on the African Coast in Accordance with Humane Principles and With the Laws of Revealed Religion*; in 1852 the Rev. Josiah Priest published *A Bible Defense of Slavery*, while C. Carroll (1900) in his work *The Negro a Beast* or *In the Image of God* includes a chapter ("Biblical and Scientific Proofs that the Negro is Not a Member of the Human Race") in which he asserts that all scientific research confirms his [the Negro] typically simian [characteristic of apes or monkeys [2]] nature. [3] Mr. Carroll asserted "that the Negro and the lower apes and four-footed animals all belong to one kind of flesh, the flesh of beasts."

The Negro a Beast or *In the Image of God* was hailed as "the reasoner of the age, the revelator of the century! The Bible as it is!

The negro and his relation to the human family!" [4]

'They are not human beings. If they come close to me, I'll kill them. I'll blow their faces to pieces.' That was what a white South African said about blacks when he was being interviewed on the CBS six o'clock Evening News on February 15, 1990. The man, an Afrikaner, made that statement in reponse to a question about the possibility of integrating South African Society now that Nelson Mandela has been released from prison after spending about twenty-seven years in confinement.

Are the opinions expressed by the Afrikaner and by those writers now a dead ember, or an abiding issue in the forefront or in the recess of the minds of people around the globe?

And what do we find in the society today about racial discrimination?

THE CURSE AND SOCIETY TODAY

Millions of people living in nations professing to be Christian still believe that blacks were cursed by God, and thus inferior. James Farmer, founder and former National Director, Congress of Racial Equality, Washington, D.C., wrote:

> Slavery was a profitable economic institution, but somehow it didn't seem moral. Many people, therefore, sought to justify it through religious doctrine. Some theologians of the early slave period used the story of God's curse on Ham and the children of Ham, supposedly the ancestry of the Africans. The early New England Calvinists distorted Calvin's theory of predestination, saying that Blacks were unelect of God, predestined to be slaves.[5]

The book *Science and the Concept of Race* made this observation about the curse: "It is instructive . . . to note that in the nineteenth-century endeavor to eliminate slavery, strong use was made of theology, then still dominant in the realm of ideology. There was also a strong pro-slavery position couched in theological terms and specifically based on *biblical interpretations.*" [6] The book further said that "such arguments [that blacks were cursed by God] still survive." [7]

Almost all black nations have been colonized. Blacks have been subjected to inhumane slavery in the Americas, oppressed in Britain, and slaughtered even in their native lands, among which South Africa is an outrageous example. Is not all that to be interpreted as a fulfillment of the curse by God?

Blacks living in the U.S. are at the mercy of white Americans.

An African is held for a slave ship. The first black slaves were sent to the New World in the early 16th century. *(The Granger Collection.)*

Slave trade on the coast of Africa. *(The Bettmann Archive.)*

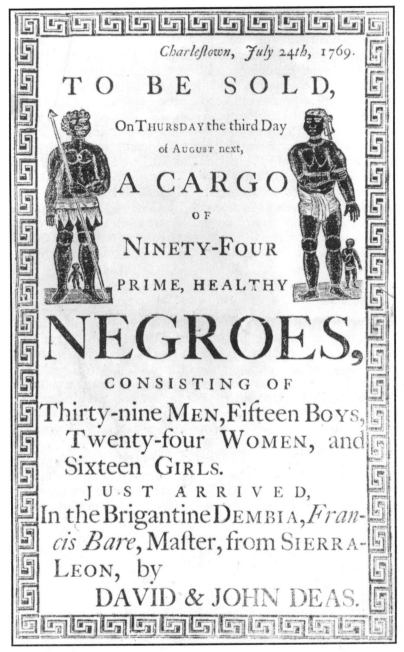

Broadside for Charleston, S.C., slave auction in 1769. *(The Granger Collection.)*

Blacks living in Britain are at the mercy of white British. Blacks living in south Africa are at the mercy of white South Africans. Black South Africans rely heavily on white governments, especially the U.S., for their freedom. Nations dominated by blacks depend on white technology. If all that does not mean that blacks were meant to be servants to whites, what does it mean?

The many languages spoken in Africa and in other parts of the world in which blacks live have caused disunity and weakness among blacks. Tribalism has also caused confusion and bloodshed among blacks. Because many predominantly white nations are not suffering from the turmoil caused by scores of languages and tribalism existing among blacks, is that an indication that God wanted whites to subjugate blacks? Did blackness of skin come about as a result of a curse by God, as some people have asserted? Also, and very importantly, are blacks backward scientifically and technologically because they were cursed by God?

Here now are a few examples of discrimination in recent times.

SOCIETY AND RACIAL DISCRIMINATION

Husband: Ron Allen, white. Wife: Toni Jo Allen, white. They were blessed with a daughter named Ariene.[8] Toni Jo divorced her husband and married a black man, Jim Brown. Normally, the custody of Ariene should have been granted to her mother, but a state judge granted custody of the little girl to her white father.

There is no reason why a judge cannot grant the custody of a girl to her father, provided there are legal or moral reasons for doing so. But why did Judge Morrison Buck of Tampa, Florida, grant the custody of Ariene to her father? Was there a moral or legal ground for the choice of custody of the girl?

"Despite the strides that have been made," said Judge Buck, "in bettering relations between the races in this country, it is inevitable that [Ariene] will, if allowed to remain in her present situation [with her mother who was married to a black man], suffer from social stigmatization that is sure to come." [9]

Declaring that the child was wrongly taken from her mother and stepfather, Chief Justice Warren Burger said: "Private biases may be outside the reach of the law, but the law cannot, directly or indirectly, give them effect. It is clear that the outcome [of the custody case] would have been different had she [Mrs. Brown] married a caucasian male of similar respectability. The Constitution cannot control such prejudices but neither can it tolerate them." [10]

The gangrene of racial prejudice is spreading in many other

ways. Some of these may surprise you, especially in this day and age. Here are two examples: Recently, a passenger of an airline in the United States said to a black steward: "I don't want a nigger to serve me."

Branding slaves on the coast of Africa previous to embarkation. *(The Bettmann Archive.)*

British soldiers mortally wounding Crispus Attucks, an Afro-American, in the Boston Massacre of 1770.

The crew of the airline had moral strength to say: "If you don't want a nigger to serve you, you are not getting any service."

In Marshall, Virginia, the proprietors of a restaurant refused to serve blacks.[11] That takes us back to the time when blacks could not eat in a restaurant with whites, and those who ventured to do so had soup, gravy and other food items poured on their heads as others cheered on! We are also reminded of the time blacks could not ride a bus with whites, or attend the same movie theatre with whites.

Richard Threlkeld (an ABC Senior News Correspondent) made this observation about Selma, Alabama: "Everything has changed; yet nothing has changed."

What Mr. Threlkeld was saying was that rights for blacks exist; discrimination has been outlawed. Yet discrimination in all its ugly forms is still being practiced.

A man in Alabama said that the slavery chain has not been broken, it has only become invisible. He had good reasons for making the statement, and the economic disparity between whites and blacks is one of them. The black man can now ride in the bus with the white man, but no black man owns a bus company. The black man can now eat lunch in a restaurant with the white man, but, in many cases, the black man cannot afford the lunch.

It is also believed that equality of blacks with whites is now more elusive than ever before. In 1984, for example, there were twice as many blacks in poverty as whites (whites, eleven percent; blacks, thirty-eight percent), yet blacks constitute less than twelve percent of the current U.S. population.[12]

A current report by National Urban League says that it would take fifty-four years for blacks to reach equality with whites in managerial and professional jobs, and seventy-three years to reach average earnings with whites and undetermined amount of time for family income to climb to that of whites and 159 years before black poverty rates diminish to those of whites.

The most mind-boggling of it all is this: It would not be until the year 3152 that the black rate of home-ownership can reach a par with that of whites. We are talking about 1,613 years from now!

The reason given for this great disparity: "institutional racism" being practiced by mortgage lenders, housing developers and real estate agents.[13]

The effect of poverty is more devastating to infants than to adults. In Harlem, the infant mortality rate is currently reported to be twice that of the nation. This means that blacks' conditions have not significantly changed in many aspects in almost 30 years.

The book *The Concept of Race* confirms that statement: "In 1958 the death rate of Negroes in the first year of life was fifty-two per thousand, and for whites, twenty-six. Thousands of infants died unnecessarily." [14]

Harlem, you might say, that is not a fair example. "We all know Harlem. Squalid! Come on now, be fair." Okay. Neither are Watts in Los Angeles, Queens in New York, Pensacola or Tallahassee in Florida true pictures of the black infant mortality in the U.S. So we will use the whole nation as an example. Fair?

More than one out of every two black children in the U.S. lives below the poverty level. That is according to a 1984 report. A 1985 report from the Department of Health and Human Services put preventable or excess black infant mortality at 6,100 a year. That is a rate of 16.7 fatalities a day.

According to the 300-page report put out by Children's Defense Fund, the condition of minority infants in the U.S. is pathetic. The Fund's president, Marian Wright Edelman, told a news conference on January 16, 1986: "The nation's progress since 1965 in improving key health indicators for poor non-white mothers and babies has ground to a virtual halt."

The report says that the black infant mortality rate is twice that of whites, and that the gap of infant mortality between the two color groups is the widest in forty years.

Calling the condition shameful, Edelman said, "A black infant in Chicago, Cleveland or Detroit is more likely to die in the first year of life than an infant in Costa Rica." (Infant mortality rate in Costa Rica is currently at 24.2 for every 1,000 live births.)

So there is one nation, but two separate classes: black and white, separate and unequal.

It must be said, however, that there are poor whites and a handful of relatively well-to-do blacks.

Nonetheless, you may wonder why such a high rate of infant poverty does not cause a ripple in the affairs of society. We will be hard-pressed to find a better answer than what is said on this matter in the same book, *The Concept of Race*: "A lynching stirs the whole community to action, yet only a single life is lost. Discrimination, through denying education, medical care, and economic progress, kills at a far higher rate. A ghetto of hatred kills more surely than a concentration camp, *because it kills by accepted custom*, and it kills every day in the year." [15]

There is more to the wretched situation. The following table is a comparison of longevity of blacks and whites.

YEAR	WHITE		BLACK	
	MALE	FEMALE	MALE	FEMALE
1971	67.9	75.5	61.6	69.8
1975	69.5	77.3	62.4	71.3
1980	70.7	78.1	63.8	72.5
1985	71.9	78.7	65.3	75.3 [16]

Margaret M. Heckler, health and Human Services Secretary, says: "Although tremendous strides have been made in improving the health and longevity of the American people, significant health inequalities still exist among members of racial and ethnic minority groups." [17] Secretary Heckler's report shows that more than 60,000 deaths could be avoided each year if mortality rates for blacks and other minority groups were as low as the rates for whites. In other words, inequalities in health care due to race will kill 164 Americans each day.

The president of Children's Defense Fund, Marian Wright Edelman, had this to say on maternal and child health status in the U.S.: "For some indicators, there has been an outright reversal of progress."

John E. Jacobs, president of the Urban National League, declares the state of black Americans as still "very grim." Gary Orfield, a political scientist, states that political progress of blacks has not matched their economic opportunities. Kate Williams, a Chicago fair housing activist, says that discrimination is not just a local program, but a national one.

In the Windy City, incidents of racial discrimination seem to be blowing everywhere. Here are two instances: A black woman living in a predominantly white neighborhood had her telephone line cut, utility line disconnected, and her tires slashed. A black couple who rented an apartment from a bank in a white neighborhood had to flee for their lives. Their apartment was pelted with stones by a mob; windows were broken and other acts of vandalism were committed. It was a nightmare in broad daylight for the couple and their little boy.

Had the woman and the couple disturbed the peace in their neighborhood? No. They had hardly moved in before terror started to rain on them.

On November 30, 1985, police arrested thirty-four demonstrators in southwest Philadelphia who were demonstrating against blacks moving into a predominantly white neighborhood. About a week earlier there had been two demonstrations of 200 and 300 strong, protesting against an interracial couple who had moved into the same neighborhood. The demonstrators chanted: "We want them out" and "beat it." Many black-tenanted houses were firebombed.

It has been said that racial unrest in Chicago is as tense now as when Dr. King marched there more than twenty years ago.

The storm of racial discrimination was swirling in the city offices of Chicago as well and polarized (at least for a while) the late Mayor Harold Washington and some city officials. They had heated arguments a few times. Are you surprised that such racial incidents bedeviled the offices of the city of Chicago? No, not if you knew about the tense racial tone that dominated the city when two candidates of distinctly different colors of skin were campaigning for the office of mayor.

RACIAL UNREST IN BRITAIN

The banner of bigotry has also been hoisted against minority groups in Britain. *The U.S. News & World Report* of July 20 and 27, 1981, made this observation about racial turmoil in England: "Experts agreed that the underlying cause of the violence was racial tension, exacerbated [or aggravated] by worsening economic crisis." [18]

"Explanations [for the violence] range from surging unemployment to racism.[19] Victor Hausner, director of inner research programs at the Economic and Social Research Council of London, said: "If you mix highly concentrated deprived areas with people piled on top of each other in public housing, and you add high unemployment and racial problems, there is bound to be trouble." [20] *America* of September 26, 1981, reported: "Britain is a multiracial society with a good deal of hatred." [21]

The police are also implicated in racism practiced in England. According to the same *Los Angeles Times* edition, Bernie Grant, who heads one of London's thirty-two borough governments, ". . . complained bitterly about police harassment of blacks. He accused law enforcement authorities of practicing overt, aggressive racism that has steadily worsened." [22]

Lord Scarman, a senior judge commissioned by the government to find the underlying reasons for racial tension in Britain, said that racial disadvantages and discrimination have not been eliminated in British society, and that racial discrimination "will continue to be a portent factor of unrest." [23]

Racism is, of course, an institutionalized evil in South Africa. That it has claimed the lives of thousands is known worldwide.

WHAT PEOPLE THINK

It seems proper, at this stage, to find out what people—blacks and whites—think about the idea that blacks were cursed by God.

I took the question to a white American friend of mine. "Do you think," I asked, "that white Americans believe black people were cursed by God?"

Smiling wryly under the glitter of bespectacled eyes, he countered, "Do you really want me to tell you what white Americans think?"

"Yes, go ahead," I replied.

"They [blacks] were cursed by God," he said. "That is what white Americans believe."

I did not end the matter there. At least a black man's opinion must be heard.

One day, while working on this book in the local library, I asked a black American if he thought black people were cursed. As I was finishing the question, his eyes lighted up, opened wide, and remained unblinking.

He started to nod his head, indicating a complete agreement, and then said pensively, "Yes, I believe so. I believe they were cursed by God. I really do."

Later, as I was exiting from a pizza parlor, a man, almost out of nowhere, called, "Hi, brother! Where did you come from? The Islands?"

"No," I replied, "I am from heaven."

"Come on now, you're not," he said, as he put his hand on my shoulder.

"Well," I said, "if you don't believe that I am from heaven, would you believe me if I said I am from Africa?"

"Really?" he exclaimed. "Where in Africa do you come from? South Africa?" he asked.

"I am from Nigeria," I replied.

Then the man continued, "I hope you don't mind me stopping you like that, but you have an accent. I don't, but I am supposed to have an accent like you. You see, they brought us here as slaves. They say God put a curse on black people to be slaves. I don't know if it is true. All I know is that I am not supposed to be here. I am supposed to be over there. (Some might ask, "Who is stopping him from moving to Africa? Ship them there—wives, children and all!")

The man left in a good mood when I told him that, to me, he had an accent, and in fact, almost everybody around sounded like a foreigner.

There may be blacks who are not sure whether or not they were cursed by God. There may be blacks who definitely believe that they were not cursed. And there may be others who have never given serious thought to the matter of the curse. Nonetheless, there are hardly any blacks who have not dwelt on their status in the world as a color group. And in many countries, especially in Britain, the U.S. and South Africa, blacks' rights and their general lot in life are far behind that of society in general.

DO YOU DISCRIMINATE?

I do. Although the word discrimination has overpoweringly negative implications, it also has positive sides to it. As you know, the meaning of the word "discriminate" depends upon the context in which it is used. A person can, for instance, be discriminatory

Zanzaibar: African natives lined up by slave hunters, yoked and deported. *(The Bettmann Archive.)*

Bringing in slaves to the Shaka market. *(The Bettmann Archive.)*

about what he eats, drinks, wears, reads, watches on television, or does for recreation. A professional wine taster must have a discriminating palate, otherwise he would be out of a job. So implicit in those meanings of discrimination are sound judgment, discretion, discernment and distinction of one thing from another.

But why do people discriminate against blacks, such as is common in the U.S., Britain and South Africa? Are there genuine reasons for being prejudiced against them?

Why Do People Discriminate Against Blacks?

We must admit that discrimination is everywhere: among people of the same color of skin and of different colors of skin, among people speaking the same language or different languages, among people of different cultures or religion. However, among color groups, it seems that blacks have had more than their fair share of discrimination. Yet discrimination and oppression against them seems unrelenting. Why?

Some of the reasons people use to justify intolerance of blacks include the following: being cursed by God, as already noted, inferiority, promiscuity, neighborhoods run down for lack of care (resulting in depreciation of property), and that blacks are noisy.

One may not be able to do much about mental inferiority. It is, however, proper to find out why a person is mentally inferior, if, in fact, he is. But as for the other three reasons mentioned in the previous paragraph, they are well-taken. A person with any sense of decency or self-respect would not want to live in a squalid, promiscuous and noisy neighborhood. Many blacks are guilty of all those negative points. In fact, black teenage pregnancy out of wedlock in the U.S. was reported to be twice that of whites, and that contributes to the reasons why the U.S. has the highest rate of teenage pregnancy out of wedlock of any industrialized society.

It must be admitted, however, that other colors are not paragons of virtue in all areas of life, including those three negative points in which blacks are strikingly guilty. But why do blacks living in predominantly white societies seem to be more guilty of those social ills than others? We will see in a later chapter.

We will also examine other problems facing blacks living in the U.S., including the reasons behind family disarray and the disproportionately high rate of divorce among blacks. The rate of divorce among blacks as an ethnic group in American society is, according to *Encyclopedia Americana*, 1979, "One and a half times as great as whites. Adequate explanation for the racial difference in divorce rates is not available."

The *New York Times* says that the divorce rate among black Americans is more than double that of Hispanics and whites.[24]

In addition, we will consider how social unrest has affected the health of black Americans, especially in regards to the inordinate incidence of hypertension ("the silent killer") among blacks. A 1985 report from the U.S. Department of Health and Human Services says: "Black males under age forty-five are ten times more likely to die from hypertension than white males." [25]

In the course of my research, I have discovered that racial turmoil has a crucial effect on brain development and function. I have also found that 'social agitation' does not affect the brain development and function of a female to the same degree as it affects the brain of a male. The effect social unrest has on brain development and function of male and female black Americans is discussed. Finally, do people really hate colors of skin? My findings may leave you stunned!

RACISM AND PUBLIC AWARENESS

If racial discrimination is truly as bad in the U.S. as we have portrayed it, you may wonder why it is not as hot a public issue as it was in the 60s and 70s. Before we examine why it is not so, we must say that local television stations regularly feature alleged incidents of racial discrimination or unrest, especially at schools, between police and minority groups. The three U.S. major networks—ABC, CBS and NBC—have had special reports in their news broadcasts about the problems of racial discrimination against black Americans. (One of the networks included American Jews as a group discriminated against by some militant groups.) Reports of racial discrimination are common in the newspapers and, to a lesser degree, in magazines.

Be that as it may, racial discrimination is not as pressing an issue in the U.S. as it was in the past, for a number of reasons. First, there are no racial riots now as in the 60s and 70s. Also, racial discrimination is unlawful now. Of course, it was unlawful in the 60s and 70s, but the American public, by and large, was unwilling to accept the laws about racial equality.

For example, in 1954 the U.S. Supreme Court made public school segregation unlawful. The decision did not settle too well with most Americans, and neither did the Court's decision in 1969 ordering desegregation of public schools. In fact, a greater number of black children were attending predominantly black schools in he late 1960s than in 1954 when the Supreme Court declared school segregation unlawful. But what about now?

The current status of school desegregation is, well, let the
U.S. News & World Report of December 8, 1980 answer: "Busing
was supposed to put more black children into schools with white
children and break up the all-black or nearly all-black schools in
black neighborhoods.[26] Has busing served the purpose it was
established to serve? The same publication answers:

> But the record shows that in many cities, despite years
> of busing, one-race schools still exist. In mixed schools,
> blacks remain an overwhelming majority. Urban school
> systems, as a whole, are more heavily black than ever.
>
> Whites have become a small and steadily shrinking
> minority in schools of one big city after another. In Detroit,
> before busing began in 1971, the schools were over 60 per-
> cent black. Today they are 82 percent black. Richmond
> schools have gone from 55 percent white to 82 percent
> black, and Boston schools from 60 percent white to 60 per-
> cent black since busing began in those cities.[27]

And what of the nation's capital, where national decisions are
made? "In Washington, D.C., since integration," says *U.S. News
& World Report*, "black enrollment has shot up from 57 percent to
96 percent, and in Atlanta, schools that were 59 percent white are
now 90 percent black." [28] In other words, as more blacks were
bused to a school in order to integrate with whites, whites moved
out of the school. As a result, the school ended up having more
black students and fewer white students than before busing was
introduced.

Those are just a few examples out of many showing that discrimination, even on the educational level, is on the rise. If discrimination is unlawful, why is it on the rise? Because the law
itself does not, and cannot, stop racial discrimination; it merely
makes it *unlawful*. If you, for example, are not prejudiced against
any race, is it because you read it in the law book? Whereas those
who are versed in law, or are even lawmakers, may be bigoted!

It is as Chief Justice Burger said: "Private biases may be outside the reach of the law. The Constitution cannot control . . .
prejudices."

In fact, many try to circumvent the law, especially when it
comes to hiring blacks. The *laws* against discrimination may be in
the book, but as for *discrimination* itself, it is business as usual.

Another reason why racial agitation does not dominate the
news in the U.S. is that it is now centralized into organizations
fighting for the rights of minority groups. These organizations
include the Urban League, Affirmative Action and the National

Association for the Advancement of Colored People (NAACP). Furthermore, the law makes provisions for people to sue for gross racial injustice. Instead of fighting for their rights in the streets, those who feel they are grossly discriminated against are fighting in the courtrooms.

Many individuals or minority groups have taken the police department to court on the grounds of unwarranted police brutality. For instance, the couple who were stoned out of their apartment have reportedly sued the city of Chicago for lack of police protection from violent racists. In the past, blacks did not have a right to sue.

Probably the most important reason why racial riots have not ravaged the cities and towns of the U.S. (and the potential for racial riots is there) is because of high unemployment rates among blacks, whites and other minority groups in recent times.

Discrimination in employment has also affected other minority groups in the United States. Asians, Cubans and Mexicans are among these. They are accused of taking jobs from blacks and whites. *U.S. News & World Report* had this to say about a black educator living in Miami: "When my family moved here in 1950, the vast majority of the skycaps, waiters and barbers were black. Now most are Latin." [29] The Asians and Latinos are also the subject of racial discrimination in other cities, including Los Angeles and New Orleans.

ONE OF THE EVILS OF THIS COUNTRY

In view of the explosive racial incidents we have experienced during the last few decades, W.E.B. DuBois was very accurate when he predicted in 1903 that: "The problem of the twentieth century will be the problem of color line: of the relations between the lighter and darker peoples of the earth in Asia and Africa, in America [and Europe] and the Islands of the Sea." [30]

However, racial discrimination cannot go on unchecked. There are many reasons for this. Ruth Benedict mentions some of them in her book, *Race: Science and Politics*: "Racial relations today present more dangerous features in the field of interhuman relations than any other point of conflict. Nowhere are mob passions, prejudices, and fears so easy to invoke and so difficult to check." [31] The indiscriminate killings on racial grounds in South Africa authenticate the quotation above.

Because racial relations today present more dangerous features than ever before in human history, the survival of the human race hangs in precarious balance. A civilization that will endure must begin its development with the ability to deal smoothly with fellow humans within and outside its boundaries.

But, ironically, man knows more about science and technology than he does about how to get along with his fellow humans. The ability of man to communicate through electronic devices is almost magical. Man has not only made communication with humans living in any corner of the globe easy as child's play, but he also has been able to communicate with heavenly bodies. Yet he finds it difficult to get along with fellow humans here on earth, or his neighbors, or even members of his own family.

Obviously, what we greatly need is to learn how to live peacefully with each other. Increased knowledge in the fields of science and technology will not make the world safer or people happier, unless and until we increase our tolerance of those with whom we must unavoidably share this planet.

People are unable to live peacefully with one another for several reasons. Apart from religion and politics, perhaps three important and intriguing reasons why people are blindly prejudiced are centered in these questions: (1) Do all living humans have a common ancestor? (2) If so, why are there so many varieties, especially in colors of skin? (3) Are all people equal, particularly mentally?

We will attempt to answer those questions, as well as examine religious and political actions that create racial conflict.

NOTES:

1. Ashley Montagu, *Man's Most Dangerous Myth: The Fallacy of Race* (New York, Oxford University Press, 1974) p. 19. It must be strongly emphasized that Mr. Montagu does not share this debased opinion about black people. He was merely referring to the opinion of a writer who seems to be Gomes Eannes de Azurra in his book *Chronicle of the Discovery and Conquest of Guinea.* At the footnote of *Man's Dangerous Myth*, Mr. Montagu, for whom I have great respect, said: "It was not God, but drunken Noah, who cursed Canaan the son of Ham, whose descendants occupied Africa, to be a 'servant of servants unto his brethern' " (Genesis 9). This was clearly in contradiction to the Divine Mind as expressed by Jesus of Nazareth: "One is your Master and all ye are brethren."

2. Random House Dictionary.

3. UNESCO, *The Race Question in Modern Science* (New York, Whiteside & William Morrow, 1956, p. 25

4. See National Union Catalog, Pre 1956 Imprints, Library of Congress Vol 96, 1970, p. 670, published by Roman and Littlefield, 81 Adams, Totowa, N.J. *The Negro a Beast* or In the *Image of God* was published in 1900 by American Book and Bible House, St. Louis, MO.

5. "Human Rights: A National Perspective 'If Not Now, When?',," *Today's Education*, April/May 1981, p. 12.

6. Margaret Mead, *Science and the Concept of Race*, (NY: Columbia University Press, 1968) p. 123.

7. *Ibid.* p. 123

8. Real names of those involved have been changed.

9. "Court Bars Racial Bias in Custody Cases," *San Diego Union*, 26 April 1984, p.1.

10. *Ibid.*, p.1

11. "Charges in Racial Case," *San Diego Union*, 18 Deember. 1984, p.A4.

12. Special program on ABC television network about the status of black Americans.

13. "Black Home-Ownership Pace: 1,163 Years to Catch Whites," *San Diego Tribune*, 8 August 1989, p. A3.

14. Ashley Montagu, *The Concept of Race* (New York, The Free Press of Glencoe, 1964), p. 258.

15. Montagu, p. 258.

16. Statistical abstract of the United States, 1989, p. 71.

17. "Minorities Still Seen as Lagging in Health Status," *New York Times*, 17 October, 1985, p. 16.

18. "When Racial Strife Tore Britain," *U.S. News & World Report*, 20 July 1981, p. 7.

19. "Strife Torn Britain: Looking for Answers," *Report*, 27 July 1981, p. 21.

20. "Urban Turmoil in Britain: Legacy of Mulitracialism," *Los Angeles Times*, 22 October, 1985, p. 10.

21. "British Political Theatre," *America*, 26 September 1981, p. 162.

22. *Los Angeles Times*, 22 October 1985, p. 10.

23. "Racial Wounds," *Time*, 7 December 1981, p. 44.

24. "Black Divorces Soar, Experts Cite Strains," *New York Times*, 24 May 1982, p. 17.

25. "Minorities Still Seen as Lagging in Health Status," *New York Times*, 17 October 1985, p. 16.

26. "Why So Many Say Busing is a Failure," *U.S. News & World Report*, 8 December. 1980, p.59.

27. *Ibid., Report*, p. 59.

28. *Ibid.*, p. 59.

29. "Rage in Miami: A Warning?", *U.S. News & World Report*, 2 June 1980, p.21.

30. James Farmer, "Human Rights: A National Perspective, 'If Not Now, When?'," *Today's Education*, April/May 1981, p.12.

31. Ruth Benedict, *Race: Science and Politics* (N.Y.: Viking Press, 1968), p. 139.

TWO

MANKIND—EQUAL OR NOT?

"Brooklyn-born Louis Kushnick, vice chairman of the Institute of Race Relations and lecturer at Victoria University [says]: 'There is a deep general racialism in the [British] society that is a product of the colonial political culture that said blacks were inferior, so whites had a right to rule them.' " [1]

In fact, a major reason behind the racial riots in Britain in recent years has been attributed to the views expressed in the U.S., Britain, and South Africa, that blacks are inferior to whites. Is that true?

THE THEORY OF EVOLUTION

Suppose we start our discussion about equality of man with the evolution theory. Let us say at the outset that our brief discussion about evolution is not designed to prove the theory of evolution as either true or false, rather, what we have to say about evolution will be confined to what evolutionists think about the equality of man.

Almost unanimously, evolutionists agree that all living humans are equal—scientists refer to all humans as Homo Sapiens. (We will have more to say about Homo Sapiens a little later on.) However, a few evolutionists do not believe in the equality of man. One such individual is Mr. Coon, who has expressed a belief in a separate evolutionary development of man.

The former president of the American Association of Physical Anthropologists asserted, in his book, *The Origin of Races*, that there were five races of man, and that each race evolved into Homo Sapiens separately and independently of each other. Coon claimed that the black people were the last to evolve, about 200,000 years later than white people, which is why, according to him, blacks all over the world are backward.[2]

WHAT SCIENTISTS SAY ABOUT EQUALITY OF THE HUMAN RACE

Encyclopedia Britannica says: "All living humans constitute a single biological species [Homo Sapien]. It is the species that represents a single kind of living thing. Man is a *single* species" (Vol. 15, 1978).

The World Book Encyclopedia says: "All human beings have a common ancestry. In this sense, all people related to one another . . . All existing human races—that is, all people living today—belong to the same species Homo Sapiens" (Vol. 16, 1980).

"All mankind is of the same genus, Homo, and the same species, Sapiens," declares *Encyclopedia Americana.* "Any classification is, therefore, subspecific."

The latin word "genus" means birth, race, kind or class, hence the expressions "the human race," "humankind" or "mankind." Speaking about the oneness of the human family, Dr. Ashley Montagu, one of the most respected scientists of our time, has this to say:

> All varieties of man belong to the same species and have the same ancestry. This is a conclusion to which all relevant evidence of comparative anatomy, paleontology, serology, and genetics, points. On the genetic ground alone it is virtually impossible to conceive of the varieties of man as having originated separately. Genetically, the chances against such a process ever having occurred are, in terms of probability, of such an order as to render that suggestion inadmissible. On purely physical grounds it is, again, highly improbable that starting from different ancestral stocks, the varieties of man would have independently come to resemble one another as closely as they do. This is demanding too much from convergence.[3]

Professors William C. Boyd and Isaac Asimov echo Dr. Montagu's opinion in their book, *Races and People:* "All human beings, however different they may appear to be, are members of this one species . . . what we call races are therefore, at most, like different varieties of dogs, only varieties within a single species." [4]

Professor Le Gros Clark, an eminent anatomist and physical anthropologist of Oxford University, England, made this observation about people:

At first sight, the contrast in appearance between such extreme types of mankind as the Negroid, Mongoloid and European might suggest fundamental constitutional differences. In fact, however, a close anatomical study seems to show that the physical differences are confined to quite superficial characters. I may best emphasize this by saying that if the body of a Negro were to be deprived of all superficial features such as skin, hair, nose and lips, I do not think any anatomist could say for certain, in an isolated case, whether he was dealing with the body of a Negro or a European.[5]

Also, the fact that all humans, regardless of color, can interbreed and their children can function well both physically and mentally shows that the human race is from one ancestry. Animals of different kinds, such as a horse and a cow, a dog and a lion, a bear and a buffalo, cannot successfully interbreed. In view of the foregoing, we can unequivocally say that *all humans, regardless of color, language, culture and so forth, are of the same biological makeup.*

LOGICAL PROOF OF MAN'S EQUALITY

People with all colors of skin can be educated and qualified to be doctors, lawyers, engineers, computer technicians, pilots and so forth. Students from underdeveloped countries study and master the languages of developed countries, such as German, English, French and Russian. Not only do the foreign students from technologically and scientifically backward nations master the languages of developed nations, but they also study in those languages and qualify as doctors, engineers, lawyers, and so forth. Is such ability an indication of inferiority? How many people living in the developed nations of Europe, North America or Japan, for instance, would want to study an African language and master such a language well enough to pass his doctorate degree in medicine, law, or business studies? What is more, some of those foreign students may even perform better academically than many natural citizens of technologically and scientifically advanced nations who need not master a foreign language in order to undertake their course of studies.

Furthermore, in academic fields, students of the same color of skin excel each other; students of different colors of skin excel one another. Vagaries in academic performance among people with different colors of skin and the same color are common to all schools and college campuses. Also, how do we explain the great disparity in the fields of science and technology among Europeans? The Spanish and the Portuguese are, for example, far less advanced than the northern Europeans, such as Germans, Swiss or the Swedes, Are some segments of the European society inferior to others? Are the Japanese superior to the Chinese because the Japanese are more scientifically and technologically advanced than the Chinese? Were the ancient Egyptians, ancient Chinese, and ancient Indians superior to their European contemporaries simply because those people developed advanced science and technology before the Europeans?

Incidentally, (and we are not attaching any importance to a color of skin) a black doctor discovered the system that makes blood transfusions possible; another black invented the traffic light, and another developed the modern advanced golf club. Quite appropriately, then, Benedict says: "If I were to select the most intelligent, imaginative, energetic and emotionally stable third of mankind, all races would be represented." [6]

You may wonder why racial discrimination exists in spite of all that is known about the equality of all people. What Ruth Benedict says about that is revealing: "All reputable anthropologists condemn the malignant nonsense about racial psychology which is preached and published by those who try to justify the oppression of ethnic minorities. *Political theories about race are nothing more than instruments of propaganda, devised for the child minds of totalitarian populations.*" [7] (Italics ours).

Even people who are well-informed about the reasons for the different colors of skin, about why some cultures are relatively backward, and about why some people seem to have resigned themselves to living in squalid conditions, may themselves be prejudiced against some races or colors of skin. Why? Because people, well-informed or not, usually dwell more upon what happened than why it happened, the appearance of poor living conditions rather than the cause, for example. This is especially true if what happened is unpleasant. Also, the reasons why a particular bad condition exists may not be obvious.

Nobody can see or touch discrimination; it is a state of mind. However, the effects can be devastating and have been confirmed all over the world. Classic examples can be found in the U.S., Britain, and South Africa. And will history ever forget what Hitler did to the Jews? In all those cases people usually dwell more on what happened than *why* it occurred.

True as that may be, the question arises: If all humans are equal in every way, why is it that many black nations are so backward scientifically and technologically? Not only do they lag behind in the fields of science and technology, they cannot even feed their people. Is that not an evidence of inferiority?

No. Incidentally, many non-black nations are not advanced scientifically and technologically. Also, it is either that people are equal or not equal. If they are all equal, as already proved scientifically and logically, they must have the inherent physical and mental capabilities to develop. Therefore, if a segment of the human race is not advanced in the fields of science and technology, it must be due to external causes, such as political instability, mismanagement of resources and superstitious beliefs. The reasons why about eighty percent of the world's population is under-developed cannot be appropriately discussed in this book.

Let us now find out what is the Bible's view about equality of all people. This is imperative because, as discussed in the last chapter, the Bible is implicated in racial discrimination.

WHAT DOES THE BIBLE SAY ABOUT THE EQUALITY OF PEOPLE?

The Bible has this to say about how the first human pair were created:

> Then the Lord said, "It is not good for the man to be alone. I will provide a partner for him." So God formed out of the ground all the wild animals and all the birds of heaven. He brought them to the man to see what he would call them, and whatever the man called each living creature, that was its name. Thus the man gave names to all cattle, to the birds of heaven, and to every wild animal; but for the man himself no partner had yet been found. And so the Lord God put the man into a trance, and while he slept, he took one of his ribs and closed the flesh over the place. The Lord God then built up the rib, which he had taken out of man, into a woman. He brought her to the man, and the man said:
>
>> "Now this, at last—
>> bone from my bones,
>> flesh from my flesh!—
>> this shall be called woman,
>> for from man was this taken."
>> (Gen. 2:18-23) (The New English Bible) [8]

As can be seen from the passage quoted, Adam did not have a mate or a helper of his kind, so God decided to create a woman, Eve, for Adam. First God caused Adam to sleep, then he took a rib-bone from Adam. From the rib-bone God created Eve. As shown in the quote, Adam and Eve then were the only human pair from which the population of the world was to spring. For the Bible says, "The man called his wife Eve because she was the mother of all who live" (Gen. 3:20). The New American Bible renders the quote this way: "because she [Eve] became the mother of all the living." The New World Translation renders the same phrase: "because she had to become the mother of everyone living."

Confirming the creation account of man thousands of years later, the record in the book of Acts says: "And hath he [God] made of *one blood* all nations of men to dwell on all the face of the earth" (King James, Acts 17:26).

The New American Bible reads: "From *one stock* he made every nation of mankind to dwell on the face of the earth."

Clearly, the Bible confirms that all mankind has a common ancestor: Adam.

Of course, for Adam and Eve to be our parents, they had to have sons and daughters. Cain and Abel were sons of Adam and Eve. However, for the population of the world to spread, Adam and Eve must also have given birth to daughters and, possibly, more sons. "Adam was one hundred and thirty years old when he begot a son in his likeness and image, and named him Seth. After the birth of Seth he lived eight hundred years, and had other *sons and daughters*" (Gen. 5:3,4).

Since there were no other humans living on the surface of the earth then, unavoidably Cain, Seth and other sons of Adam must have married their sisters. Such marriage was not incestuous then because that was the only way the world could be populated with humans. What is more, Eve was taken from Adam, as we have earlier considered. Yet, Eve was Adam's wife. In view of all this, the oneness of the human family is inseparably secured.

But as we shall see, a chapter of human history ends violently, and another begins.

A GLOBAL DELUGE

As time went on, sons and daughters of Adam became numerous on the surface of the earth. Also saturating the earth was wickedness and violence. A watery deluge of global dimensions was decided upon by God to eradicate the incorrigible practicers of unrighteousness. Biblical accounts show that Noah and members of his family were the only ones found to be "righteous" before God. Noah, under divine command and instruction, constructed the first water vessel, an ark, to preserve through the deluge specimens of land animals and members of his family.

Regarding Noah's following divine directions or specifications in building the ark, the Bible says: "Exactly as God had commanded him, so Noah did" (Gen. 6:22).

After Noah had completed the ark and had gathered specimens of land-dwelling mammals and birds into it, what happened?

"In the year when Noah was six hundred years old, on the seventeenth day of the second month, on that very day, all the springs of the great abyss broke through, the windows of the sky were opened, and rain fell on the earth for forty days and forty nights. On that very day Noah entered the ark with his sons, Shem, Ham and Japheth, his own wife, and his three sons' wives" (Gen. 7:11-13).

So, altogether, eight souls—Noah and his wife, Noah's three sons and their three wives—survived the global deluge.

Thousands of years later the Genesis account just quoted was supported in II Peter: "Nor did He spare the world in ancient times: it was only Noah He saved, the preacher of righteousness, along with seven others, when He sent the Flood over a disobedient world" (The Jerusalem Bible, II Peter 2:5).

It was from this family of eight that the world became re-populated. "The sons of Noah who came out of the ark were Shem, Ham and Japheth; Ham was the father of Canaan. These three were the sons of Noah, and their descendants spread over the whole earth" (Gen. 9:18-19). Or from the three sons of Noah "the whole world was peopled" (The New American Bible).

Since Noah was a descendant of Adam and Eve, all humans, regardless of color, language or culture, are from one and only one couple—Adam and Eve. Thus, according to the Bible, the bloodtie of man was, and still is, cemented once and for all time. The seeming differences are superficial.

As Sharon McKern puts it, "It is by understanding the facts of racial differences that scientists can prove the equality of mankind. As individuals, we differ in intelligence, abilities and special skills. But as races, we are equal. Physical anthropologists devote many years to research and study of this single area of interest. And their findings consistently bear out the truth of one fact: no race is 'superior' or 'inferior' to any other." [9]

So the Bible and science are in perfect harmony about the ancestry and equality of all people. Therefore, the equality of man is called into question only on the grounds of religious interpretation, politics, ethics, and ethnics, certainly not on biological, scientific, or even Biblical, basis.

In view of the foregoing, should we not accept with utmost

skepticism Mr. Coon's view that there were five separate evolutionary developments of mankind, and that these developments
took place independent of each other? More importantly, would
you, in view of what we have discussed, agree with Mr. Coon that
one color group could be 2,000,000 years ahead of all other colors
in their evolutionary development?

If all humans are equal, as just proved scientifically, Biblically
and logically, why does it seem as though some races are backward and generally subservient to whites? Is it because of a working curse? Does this supposed curse have anything to do with
color of skin?

NOTES

1. Marguerite Johnson, "Anger in the Streets," *The Times*, July 20, 1981, p.32.

2. C. Coon, *The Origin of Races*, (New York, NY, Knopf, 1962) p.651.

3. Dr. Ashley Montagu, (NY, Oxford University Press, 1974) p. 74.

4. William C. Boyd and Isaac Asimov, *Races and Peoples*, (NY, Abelard-Schuman, 1955) p. 21.

5. Le Gros Clark, "Fitting Man to His Environment," (New Castle, University of Newcastle upon Tyne, England, 1949) p. 19.

6. Benedict, p. 96.

7. Ibid., p. 139.

8. The New English Bible will be the basic Bible version that will be used in this book. It will be clearly indicated whenever other versions of the Bible are quoted or referred to.

9. Sharon McKern, *The Many Faces of Man,* (New York, Lothrop, Lee & Shepard, 1972) pp. 37,38.

THREE

SCIENCE, BIBLE AND SKIN COLOR

Many will raise an eyebrow if told that all living humans came from the same ancestor.

That statement itself would not create any surprise if only one basic color of people lived on the surface of the earth. But with such a great variety of cultures and colors, it seems difficult for people to accept the idea that all of us came from the same ancestor, with no group of people inferior to another.

For example, *Encyclopedia Americana* (Vol. 20, 1980) says: ". . . associated with the slave system, and an essential part of its support was an elaborate rationalization of the inferiority of Negroes and of the wisdom and justice of a slave status for them. Arguments in support of this position were drawn from history, from early ethnology, and from the *Bible*." (Italic ours).

The argument that was drawn "from early ethnology, and from the Bible," and that is used to support the status of blacks as slaves and as a cursed people, is found in Genesis:

Noah, a man of the soil, began the planting of vineyards. He drank some of the wine, became drunk and lay naked inside his tent. When Ham, father of Canaan, saw his father naked, he told his two brothers outside. So Shem and Japheth took a cloak, put it on their shoulders and walked backwards, and so covered their father's naked body; their faces were turned the other way, so that they did not see their father naked. When Noah woke from his drunken sleep, he learned what his youngest son had done to him, and said: 'Cursed be Canaan, slave of slaves shall he be to his brothers.' And he continued: 'Bless, O

Lord, the tents of Shem; may Canaan be his slave. May God extend Japheth's bounds, let him dwell in the tents of Shem, may Canaan be their slave' (Gen. 9:20).

That is the curse and the events which led to it. Millions of people around the world, including blacks themselves, believe that the curse was directed against black people and that the curse turned their skin black. Hence, many use black color as a symbol of evil and white as a symbol of purity or righteousness. The belief that the black people were cursed by God is probably stronger in the western world, which largely professes belief in the Bible, than in the eastern sector of the world, where belief in the Bible does not seem to be widespread. Nonetheless, the persistent oppression of blacks is puzzling, not only to the Occidentals, but also to the Orientals.

But what is a curse? According to Webster's Third New International Dictionary, a curse is defined, among other things, as: "A calling to deity to visit evil on one. A solemn pronouncement or invoking of doom or great evil; to utter words calculated to consign great evil; assign to an evil fate; invoke divine vengeance or anger against."

What this means is that, no matter how hard a cursed person tries, he will not succeed. No matter how intelligent he is, success will not come his way. He will, as long as the curse remains potent, be in a state of servitude. A power higher than his is at work. Can we conclude, then, that blackness of skin color, backwardness, oppression and slavery of blacks by whites in South Africa and North America and Britain are the result of a curse by God, as we have just read from the Bible? What do the facts show?

BLACKNESS OF SKIN

In the quotation from the Bible, there is no mention of skin color or black skin resulting from a curse. Also, there are people who are not regarded as "Negroes" who have black skin. For example, many Egyptians, the Australian Aborigines, many Asian Indians, especially to the South, the Indonesians, the Pakistanis, the Negritoes (Little Blacks) of the Philippines have black, brown or yellow skin color. Southern Europeans, including Spanish, Portuguese and Southern Italians, have brown or dark skins. They are not racially classified as "Negroes."

In fact, the Asian Indians, the Pakistanis and the Iranians are genealogically linked with the Europeans. Hence the expression, "Indo-Europeans," "Indo-European Languages" or "Indo-Iranian

Languages." These expressions indicate that the Europeans migrated from Asia and that they inherited their languages—such as Germanic languages, which include English—from Asia. Yet most Europeans have lighter skin than their Asian counterparts.

Nonetheless, this question still bobbles up for an answer: If black skin is not a result of damnation by God, why then does a segment of the human race have black skin? Why are black people black?

CLIMATE AND SKIN COLOR

Varieties of skin color exist, not only among the races, but also among individuals who claim to belong to the same race. For example, all blacks are not of the same shade, nor are all whites of the same shade. Having said that, we need to draw our attention to one vital point: (The colder the climate, the lighter the skin; the hotter the climate, the darker the skin.) (Exceptions to this rule are found in Eskimos living in very cold climates and whites living in very hot climates, which we will discuss later.) The correlation of climate to skin color is not accidental.

Let us take Italy as an example. There are more incidences of blond hair and blue eyes in Northern Italy where it is cold than in Southern Italy where it is warm. What applies to Southern Italians about skin color is also true of other Southern European countries, such as Greece, Portugal, Spain, Malta and Albania. Orientals are well known for having black hair and brown eyes, but that is not totally true. If, for instance, you visit Korea you will find that there are blondes with blue eyes in Northern Korea where it is cold, but blond hair and blue eyes are rare in Southern Korea where it is warmer. People living in Southern China and Japan are darker than people living in the northern regions of these countries. Even in the U.S. people living in Southern California, Texas and Florida tend to be more brownish in color than their northern counterparts, and so are South African whites. Part of Northern Australia lies in the tropics. The average temperature year-round is 85 degrees fahrenheit (29 degrees celsius). People living in this region expose themselves a lot and tend to be brownish in color.

In addition to the part which the sun plays in the pigmentation of the skin, what else is involved?

The chief pigmenting substance in the human body is melanin. Melanin is a Greek word meaning "black." (It is from this word that the word Melanesia—"Black Islands"—was derived.) Melanin is a dark organic coloring matter present in the skin of *all normal human beings*. However, the amount of melanin varies from person to person. This is why skin colors range from very white—blondes and redheads—to very dark—ebony in some cases.

More melanin is present in the skin of black people, but all blacks are not of the same shade. Clear black, ebony-black, blue black, brown, copper-brown and yellow are some of the colors found among those classified as blacks. Observe people around you who claim to be of the same color of skin—Caucasians, Orientals, Mexicans and Blacks—and you will find how elusive it is to label a people as belonging to a color without some arbitrariness coming into play.

Please note that we are *not* saying that blacks have more melanin in their *bodies* than whites. Rather, we are saying *more melanin is present in the skin* of blacks than that of whites. What is the reason for this vital difference?

Dr. Ashley Montagu made this interesting and scientifically established observation:

> The pigmentary difference is *not* one of a kind in the skins of *all* human beings (with the exception of albinos, who have no pigment at all), varying only in its diffusion throughout the body rather than in quality.[1]

> The principal pigment, melanin, is produced in pigment cells known as melanocytes, by a reaction between amino acid tyrosine and oxygen. The enzyme tyrosinase in the melanocytes acts on tyrosine to produce and control the speed of production of melanin. Exposure to ultra-violet rays of sunlight, for example, activates tyrosine into melanin. *There are no differences in the number of melanocytes in the different ethnic groups.*[2]

As mentioned in the above quotation, exposure to the ultraviolet rays of the sun "activates tyrosine to convert tyrosine into melanin." Prolonged exposure to the sun will therefore increase the production of melanin in the body, so that a white or a yellow person can turn dark, black, or to quote scientist, "ebony-black." Of course, those with more melanin in their skins, such as brunettes, will turn darker quicker than blondes or redheads.

We can appreciate this better if we stop to think of whites who work in the open, such as farmers or construction workers, and those who regularly sunbathe, usually turn dark or brown. That is also why Europeans who live in relatively warm climates of Mediterranean Europe generally have yellowish, brownish or olive colors of skin. Furthermore, since those who regularly sunbathe cannot, for the sake of decency, divest themselves completely of clothes, areas of the body that are usually covered normally remain lighter than the rest of the body that is exposed to the sun. Why so? Simply because the sun's ultraviolet rays cannot penetrate the covered areas of the body to the degree where the melanin in the skin can pigment those parts of the body.

So, we can agree with Dr. Montagu when he says, "It is not altogether an accident that we find dark skins associated with regions of high temperatures and intense sunlight and light skins with cooler climates and moderate degrees of sunlight." [3] Of course, medium light skin, as already discussed, is associated with medium cold climates.

Before we proceed any further, it seems appropriate here to mention that a black person can suffer from melanosis. Melanosis (a Greek word taken from melanin) is a condition where there are abnormal or excessive pigmentary deposits in the skin, often due to disorder in the skin metabolic mechanism. Such strong pigmentation is not the result of a double-dose of a Biblical curse, but melanosis—the extreme opposite of an albino.

If we ended our discussion about color of skin here, you might feel unconvinced because of the exceptions to the rule of climate equals skin color. If climate plays a major role in the pigmentation of the skin, why have not the whites living in hot climates turned black? Why have not the blacks living in cold climates turned white? The Eskimos would be the whitest, for they live in a very cold climate. Why have they not turned snowy white?

White to Black?

If exposure to the sun is the main determinant of pigmentation of the skin, why, then, have not whites living in hot climates of the world turned black? Simply because prolonged exposure to the sun has not taken place. Pigmentation of the skin is an extremely slow process. It would take several lifetimes of sustained exposure for a person to turn permanently black. Moreover, white people who live in hot climates do not usually expose their bodies fully to the sun's ultraviolet rays. They are mostly fully clothed, and those who open themselves to the sun to a maximum degree turn dark or brown to that degree.

For these reasons, and others that we will discuss later, whites living in hot climates have not turned black. Many of them, though, have brownish or yellowish looking skins. Many Australians fall into this category. I have seen at least two men in California who are white but have sunbathed themselves black, although whether they have actually changed their skin pigmentation is not proven.

But it has been scientifically established that "many members of the 'White Race,' without enough melanin in the skin for protection, can develop additional melanin with time if they work and play with skin exposed to the sun. (This development is rather slow, and that is why over-exposure at first will cause sunburn.) Still, many sun-tanned members of the 'White Race' actually have *more melanin* in their skin than many African members of the 'Black Race.' " [4]

For example, the Tamils of South India are darker in skin pigmentation than many black Africans. Yet the Tamils are genealogically classified as Caucasoid, often referred to as Indo-Europeans.

BLACK TO WHITE?

Since the sun is the main pigmenting factor of the skin, why have not black people living in cold climates gradually turned white because of lack of prolonged exposure to the ultraviolet rays of the sun? To answer that question, let us propound counter questions: Why is it that whites living in cold climates have not become progressively whiter over the years because of not being so much exposed to the sun's rays? Why is it that blacks living in hot climates have not developed blacker skin because of perennial exposure to the sun? Why do the skin colors of the two different climatic dwellers remain basically the same over the centuries? The answer simply lies in the fact that the melanin in the bodies of black people living in cold climates has fully developed, or has reached a saturation point. Therefore, their pigmentation remains stagnant regardless of climatic conditions. It cannot change any more than one can unripen a fruit. So blacks who do not intermarry with other colors will always remain black, whether or not they live in cold climates. Or as Nipsy Russell once said: "Once you go black, you never go back."

By the same token, a Southern Italian, a Portuguese, or a Spaniard who lives in New York will not become progressively whiter just because he now lives where it is much colder than in Southern Europe. And, of course, a white person who lives in a cold climate will not get gradually whiter simply because he lives in cold climatic conditions all his life. As we have noted, a white person can get dark. His pigmentation has not developed; it is dormant.

Obviously, one reaches a point where one can get no darker or lighter, regardless of exposure to the sun or lack of it.

ESKIMOS AND PIGMENTATION

Now the Eskimos. First of all, the Eskimos were from Asia, so they had yellow skin before migrating to the Arctics. Moreover, during six months of wintry weather in the arctics, exposure to bitter cold is usually minimal. On the other hand, exposure to the sun during the almost six months of daylight in the arctic summer is maximal. While the temperature in winter could be as low as -76°F. in Alaska (and winter temperature has been reported to be as low as -126.9°F. in Vostok), the summer temperature can be as high as 100°F. During this period, brisk activity among the arctic dwellers is at its peak and, inevitably for many, exposure to the sun is also maximum. Hence the Eskimos can maintain, over the centuries or millenniums, their pigmentation, though with some light variations: That is, there are some Eskimos whose skin color is marginally darker than Northern Europeans, but the Eskimos' skin color is invariably lighter than Southern Europeans, such as the Portuguese, the Albanians, or the Maltese.

That the sun is the chief agent that activates the human body to produce pigmentation seems confirmed in the Bible itself. About the beautiful Shulamite maiden that King Solomon had the temerity to woo, we are informed: "Look not upon me, because I am black, because the sun hath looked upon me: my mother's children were angry with me; they made me the keeper of the vineyards; but my own vineyard have I not kept" (Sol. 1:6 - AV). Obviously, the Shulamite girl's brothers or sisters, because they were angry with her, punished her by making her stay in the sun to care for their vineyards or those of the family. Consequently, she got "black" or swarthy. It must be said, however, that the Shulamite girl's pigmentation may have been superficial. Nonetheless, it was caused by the sun's ultraviolet rays.

THE EARLY MAN

Moreover, and very importantly, it is agreed upon by almost all secular authorities, especially anthropologists, archaeologists, and historians, as well as in Biblical accounts, that at his inception, man started off as a farmer, hunter, gatherer of wild fruits, berries and roots. But at some point in human history, people migrated to different parts of the world from a central location in Sumeria or ancient Babylon—"the cradle of civilization." Some migrated to cold regions, others to moderately cold climates, and still others to the tropics—the rain forests.

Surely, exposure to the sun's ultraviolet rays would be maximum for those who migrated to the tropical regions of the world, medium for those who migrated to moderate climates—such as found in most of Asia—and minimal for those who migrated to cold regions of the world, mostly Europe, the Soviet Union and most of North America. How much of one's skin is exposed to the sun depends on how one dresses. Skin pigmentation would accelerate among hot climate dwellers because they fully expose themselves to the sun(Exposure to the sun would be medium among medium climatic dwellers; therefore, their skin colors remain yellow or olive. Since full exposure to the sun (except in summer) has hardly ever been at a maximum in temperate regions of the world, the skin pigmentation of cold climatic dwellers has remained basically the same for a long time.)

What is more, hot climatic dwellers still expose themselves generously to the sun, whereas cold climatic dwellers, mostly whites, can expose themselves to the sun only in summer. Even then, they usually sunbathe with the aid of protective creams and suntan lotions, because the sun can dry up the skin and cause cancer. However, if they work and sweat in the sun, there will hardly be any need for the application of skin lotion, yet, the skin may not develop cancer. (Can you imagine an African or an Amazonian farmer giving himself a good coat of sun lotion before cultivating the soil!) At the same time, such one working and sweating in the sun will be developing skin pigmentation very slowly.

EUROPEANS IN HOT CLIMATE AND INDUSTRIAL REVOLUTION

One point is very important about skin pigmentation. It must be remembered that the Europeans emigrated to some hot climatic regions of the world *after* the advent of the Industrial and Agricultural Revolutions. For example, although Portuguese sailors discovered South Africa in 1488, it was not until 1652 that a trickle of Dutch farmers (Boers) started to settle in South Africa. The first British settlers arrived in South Africa in 1820.

What does that have to do with color of skin? What this shows is that the Industrial and Agricultural Revolutions had already taken place (in 1709) before Europeans started to emigrate into warm climatic regions of the world. (The search for raw industrial materials played a dominant role in the venture). Centuries before the Industrial Revolution, machines had been used by the Europeans in many of their undertakings, and by 1709, the application of technology to all facets of industrial and agricultural undertakings was comprehensive.

Because the Europeans imported the use of technology into

the hot climates in which they settled, the need for them to labor in searing heat was minimal, whereas the natives of these regions of the world had been doing primitive farming in parching heat from time immemorial. They had, therefore, developed skin pigmentation long before the advent of European settlers and their mechanized farming.

Furthermore, early European settlers in many hot climatic regions of the world were from Southern Europe. The countries which they colonized include Brazil (colonized by the Portuguese), and Mexico and Argentina (colonized by Spain). Concentrated emigration of other Europeans into those countries took place mainly during the late 19th century and early 20th century.

If the ancestors of the white segment of the human race had migrated to the hot climatic regions of the world, those who are white now might be black—Red heads and blonds would be yellow-black, brunettes would be brown, and most of those with black hair would be clear-black or ebony-black.

On the other hand, if the ancestors of the black segment of the human race had originally migrated to the cold climatic regions of the world, those who are black now might have been white instead. Blacks with fair skin (yellow) would either have red hair or blond, those with brown skin would be brunettes, and those who are plain black would be white with black, wavy hair. There are, of course, several other shades of blacks and whites, but those colors mentioned are basic.

Finally, the Asians, a dominantly yellow people because they live in mostly medium-cold climates, would either be blacks or whites, depending on the type of climatic region to which their ancestors had migrated.

WHY THE SKIN NEEDS TO BE PIGMENTED

The skin needs to be pigmented with melanin in order to prevent the cells in the body, especially those at the outer layers of the skin, from being damaged by the ultraviolet rays of the sun. Excessive radiation, such as used to treat cancer patients, destroy healthy body cells. The sun is a form of benevolent radiation when it is not intense. Hence, we talk about the sun's *radiant* energy. To prevent the sun's ultraviolet rays from destroying healthy body cells, the body produces skin pigmentation. Really, then, skin pigmentation is like developing an immunity to foreign matter—the harmful ultraviolet rays of the sun—in much the same way as the body develops immunity to contagious diseases, such as small pox or chicken pox. The sun, which can damage healthy skin cells, is also the agent that precipitates the formation of melanin which protects the skin from the damage ultraviolet rays of the sun can cause. It is that simple. If the interaction that results in skin pigmentation did not take place, all the people living in the tropics would have died of skin cancer.

At this stage, however, we are keenly interested in (a) why one working and sweating in the sun will not develop skin cancer; and (b) how skin pigmentation is formed and inherited.

SEBACEOUS GLANDS

We have mentioned before that one would be protected from the cancer-causing ultraviolet rays of the sun if one sweats while working in the sun. But how does this work?

Two of the main reasons why one can be exposed to the sun to an extraordinary degree and yet not be afflicted with skin cancer lie in the protection offered by *sebaceous glands* and the *water content* in the body.

Sebaceous glands are tiny, oil-producing glands located alongside the sacs or follicles of the root of hair on the skin. The glands are abundant throughout the body except on the palm of the hand and the soles of the feet where the skin is thicker.

Sebaceous glands secrete an oily substance (sebum) to keep the skin and the hair soft. The work of sebaceous glands can be likened to that of a lubricant that keeps an automobile or a machine well-oiled. The oily substance produced by the sebaceous glands also prevents moisture or water (maceration) to enter the body through skin ducts, and also serves as a general protection for the body, especially from bacteria.

Importantly, when the temperature of the body increases, the production of the oily substance also increases. Thus the skin is protected from harmful substances or objects, particularly the sun's ultraviolet rays.

SWEAT GLANDS

The sweat glands also play an important role in protecting the body from the damage the sun's radiant energy may inflict upon it.

There are two major kinds of sweat glands: *"eccrine"* and *"apocrine."* Eccrine glands are present all over the body, whereas apocrine glands are mainly found in the armpits, ear, chest, abdomen and genital regions. It is estimated that the combined number of sweat glands in the skin is between two and fifteen million.

Eccrine sweat glands are not only more abundant in the skin

than apocrine, but also reach deep into the blood vessels, and sometimes even deeper, especially to the "corium." ("Corium" is defined as a "dense, interlacing network of fibrous connective tissue carrying with it blood vessels, nerves, glands, and hair follicles"—or small particles of hair glands.)

This is how the sweat glands work: When the body's temperature increases the brain sends messages to the sweat glands to produce more sweat. There are about 100 sweat glands to an area about the size of an American quarter. However, there are more sweat glands in the scalp, forehead, feet, armpits, the nose and the palm of the hand. There are, for example, about 2,300 sweat glands in every square inch of the skin of the palm. That is why one usually sweats first or most profusely in those parts of the body.

As you well know, oil is thicker than water or sweat, so when both water and sebum are present on the skin, the water will flow off first. But the oil also impedes the flow of the sweat, so even more protection is offered the body from the sun. Of course, when the sweat flows off or evaporates from the body, a small amount of oil also goes along with it. But enough oil is still present on the skin to offer it good protection. The situation can be likened to an oily frying pan. Water can wash away, without scrubbing, some of the oil or grease in a frying pan, but most of the oil still remains. So it is with sweating and oily body exposed to the sun. Most of the sweat may run off or evaporate, but only a little of the protective oil is lost. Moreover, the sweat is evaporated by the sun before the oil is evaporated. Again, the body is well-protected from skin cancer.

Also, sweat moisturizes the oil glands so as to prevent occlusion—that is, prevents the sweat glands from being blocked or shut off.

As long as one is engaged in strenuous activity, the body, other things being equal, is bound to produce sweat and more oil than usual. So both the sweat and the oil will offer the body the needed protection from the sun's rays. We do not want to forget that the body is about 70 percent water, so we have plenty of water at our disposal. Long before one runs out of water, great thirst will force one to replenish. If one ignores the body's call for water, the body will break down from dehydration or heatstroke.

That strenuous activities in the sun protect the skin from cancer is proved true by comparing two occupations: construction and fishing. In spite of generous exposure to the sun, a construction worker is less likely to contract skin cancer than a fisherman. His skin is protected by sweat and the oily substance we have been talking about. On the other hand, a fisherman has a higher risk of developing skin cancer because he exposes himself to the sun with little or no sweat-producing activities.

SWEAT GLANDS—WHITE AND BLACK

An additional reason why dark-skinned people can withstand hot weather better than light-skinned is because dark-skinned people are endowed with more sweat glands. In a study conducted on ten blacks and twelve whites, it was found that sweat glands "occurred three times more abundantly in the Negroes than in the whites." [5] Copious sweat glands enable dark-skinned people to efficiently dissipate and regulate body temperature.

The difference in skin sweat glands between dark- and light-skinned peoples may have been caused by the degree of exposure to the sun. It stands to reason that if people who have light skin develop dark skin, they will develop proportionately more skin sweat glands.

All we have discussed about the skin is extremely basic. The skin is an enormously complicated and interwoven organ and performs a multitude of vital functions, such as eliminating wastes. Just as the hair that grows on the skin is intricate in its makeup, so is the pigmenting of the skin.

THE SKIN

The skin is the largest organ of the body. If it were to be spread out, an average adult's skin would cover about 18 square feet (1.7 square meters). The skin weighs about six pounds (2.7 kilograms).

The structure of the skin is far from simple. First of all, the inner layers of the skin consist of a multitude of cells placed side by side in rows. There are about fourteen to fifteen of these rows stacked vertically. The skin grows from the bottom or inner layers up. Underneath, the skin cells are somewhat round, but as they ascend to the surface, they become flatter and flatter. That same area, the size of an American quarter, which contains 100 sweat glands can also contain at least three million skin cells.

It takes about two weeks for a newly formed skin cell to ascend to the surface. Its life span on the surface is about 13 to 14 days, then it is shed through various ways, such as on bed linen, or when toweling the body after a shower or a bath.

This cell structure is true of all humans, regardless of color. The only difference is that the skin cells of dark or black people get pigmented by melanin when the cells are about to ascend to the surface. (Of course, we are all pink under the surface of the skin.) The life span of the skin on the surface is very short, and yet one usually maintains one's pigmentation. There is much more to the skin than what meets the eye.

HEREDITY OF PIGMENTATION

The pigment cells (melanocytes) that we discussed earlier would be inherent in one's offspring, so that a black couple will have black children, a yellow couple will have yellow children, etc. A white couple will normally have white children—though not necessarily the same identical shade.

At this stage, however, we have two important questions to answer. These are: (a) Why is it that a white person or couple who became dark as a result of exposure to the sun do not give birth to children who are commensurably dark? (b) How is pigmentation of the skin affected so that it can be passed on to one's offspring?

The first question first. A white person who got dark as a result of exposure to the sun does not have dark children because his or her pigmentation is superficial. Pigmentation of the skin, as already mentioned, is an extremely slow process. Moreover, one's mate may not sunbathe. Even if both parents sunbathed, it takes a long time for a change of pigmentation to show in one's children.

In answering our second question, let us first of all refresh our memories by requoting Dr. Montagu: "The principal pigment, melanin, is produced in pigment cells known as melanocytes, by a reaction between amino acid tyrosine and oxygen. The enzyme tyrosinase in the melanocytes acts on tyrosine [an amino acid] to produce and control the speed of production of melanin." [6]

Among the melanin-producing elements, tyrosinase is perhaps the most important. *Dorland's Illustrated Medical Dictionary* defines tyrosinase as "an oxidizing enzyme in animal and plant tissues which catalyzes the oxidation of tyrosine and other phenolic [organic compound] *into black pigments*." (Italics ours).

The pituitary gland also plays a vital role in how skin pigmentation is inherited.

THE PITUITARY GLAND AND THE PIGMENTATION OF THE SKIN

A pea-sized endocrine gland located at the base of the human brain, the pituitary gland, activates, influences or regulates several organs in the human body. As you may be aware, the endocrine gland secretes hormonal substances directly into the bloodstream. According to *Blakiston's Gould Medical Dictionary*, hormone is "a specific chemical product of an organ or of certain cells of an organ, transported by the blood or other body fluids, and having a specific regulatory effect upon cells remote from its origin."

The pituitary gland is hormonopoietic; that is, it is a hormone-producing gland. Not only does the pituitary gland produce and release hormonal substances into the bloodstream, but these pituitary substances also influence the function of other endocrine glands and non-endocrine organs throughout the whole human body. One of the organs which the pituitary gland greatly affects is the skin and especially its pigmentation. It also regulates sexual desire and function by inducing and controlling the production of hormones inside the male's testes.

All these elements—melanocytes, tyrosinase, enzymes, sweat glands, oxygen amino acids and the pituitary gland—interact in a complex way to produce skin pigmentation. But before the elements pigment the skin, they are regulated and synthesized by the hormone released to the body by endocrine glands, and thus become part of the makeup of the gene. If the pigmenting substances are not activated by the sun, they remain dormant.

When couples of different colors (or of the same color but of different shade) conjugate, the union of the sperm cell from the male and the egg cell from the female is also the union or the blending of the parent's colors of skin. Genetic information, including that of the skin, is regulated by deoxyribonucleic acid—commonly called DNA.

However, depending upon the dominant gene, and the lightness or darkness of the skin color of one of the parents, one color may dominate in their offspring. There may even be variations: that is, one color dominant in some offspring, and the other color dominant in others.

We can see, therefore, why black parents will pass pigmentation of the skin (hair and eyes) to their offspring. But white parents, although living in a hot climate, will still have white offspring simply because the melanin-producing cells in their bodies have not been activated enough for them to pass dark skin to their children.

Since the "same chemical pigments" are to be found in all human beings, and the number of melanocytes (melanin-forming cells) in all humans is the same, everybody has the potential to be pigmented black provided exposure to the sun's ultraviolet rays is sustained for several generations of laboring and sweating in the sun.

In conclusion, it seems obvious that for one to be permanently pigmented, dark or black, enough hormonal substances have to be released by the pituitary gland directly into the bloodstream for a long time. This will result in the development of permanent pigmentation. The pigmentation would be passed on to one's offspring, as one would pass other traits to one's children. Obviously, then, pigmentation of the skin is much more than a surface affair.

ARE WE ALL CURSED?

What can we conclude from all that has been said? *We cannot correctly say that black peoples inhabit hot climates and that white peoples inhabit cold climates. Rather, we should say that those inhabiting hot climates have developed pigmentation of the skin to the extent the climate is hot and to the extent they have exposed themselves to the sun's ultraviolet rays, and have therefore turned dark or black. And those living in cold climates maintain basically the same color of skin because of lack of sustained exposure to the sun's rays, since cold conditions strongly discourage such exposure.*

In view of our consideration of the color of skin, we hope that the young woman who lamented: "Why did God make me black?" now knows why she is black. We also earnestly wish that the seven-year-old girl mentioned at the beginning of this book would now understand why she could not scrub off black pigmentation from her skin. Lastly, we hope that black South Africans (and other blacks) who sang "Oh God, what have we done? Our only sin is the color of our skin," will have the opportunity to be enlightened by this book, if only to know that dark pigmentation is not as a result of sin.

WHY NOT EVERYBODY ONE COLOR?

Why does not everybody have identical color of skin? That would eliminate discrimination on the basis of color, would it not? But for everybody to have identical color of skin! Impossible! Undesirable! That will never happen. Why not? For one thing, the degree of exposure to the sun, which has a great deal to do with skin pigmentation, will never be the same for everybody, everywhere, for various reasons. The most fundamental reason is that it is not nature's way that everybody should have the same amount of melanin in his or her body. Why not? In the first place, there are differences in the frequencies of genes that determine the melanin in the body. Secondly, the possibilities in the human genes are virtually limitless. That is why there are no two human beings exactly the same, physically, mentally, or emotionally.

While twins may share striking physical similarities, their ways of life almost always differ. So it is with color among humans. *Shades of the same color of people know no end.* Also, as evident from other creations around us, variety was originally intended in all organic life.

VARIETY—THE NAME OF THE GAME

Suppose everybody had the same color of skin (say green), same height (5 ft 6 inches), facial features, color of hair, likes and dislikes, personalities. What if everybody liked the same color of clothes, the same style? What if everybody liked the same kind of food, prepared the same way? Would there be excitement if everybody bought the same kind of automobiles, the same color, identical equipment? And how exciting life would be if everybody liked the same kind of house, furniture, enjoyed the same recreation, or went to the same place for vacation year in, year out? In such situations of imagined sameness, human nature being what it is, boredom could very well send many to an early grave or to an asylum. In spite of virtually limitless things to do, some say they are bored! Do we not, therefore, appreciate variety in life? Variety certainly makes life interesting, satisfying and full of zest. Unfortunately, however, variety in humans, especially of colors, causes friction, segregation, discrimination, and bloody clashes.

However, how do we explain other physical differences, such as head hair, body hair, colors of eyes, and shapes of nose?

NOTES

1. Under infrared, an invisible light ray, everybody is pitch black.

2. Dr. Ashley Montagu, *Man's Most Dangerous Myth: The Fallacy of Race,* (New York, Oxford University Press, 1974) pp. 88,89.

3. *Ibid.,* p. 87

4. William C. Boyd and Isaac Asimov, *Races and People,* (New York, Abelard-Schuman, 1955), p. 47.

5. Montagu, p. 338.

6. Ibid., p. 88.

FOUR

OTHER PHYSICAL CHARACTERISTICS AND THE RACES

In addition to color of skin, other physical characteristics about fellow humans fascinate us, including different kinds of head hair, body hair, eyes, noses, lips and teeth.

HEAD HAIR

The colors of head hair include plain black, brown-black, dark-brown, brunette, blond, golden blond, red, sandy and other marginal varieties. Textures range from coarse, curly or kinky to wooly; there are short curly, tuft curly, long curly, frizzy, soft, wavy, straight, tightly spiralled or "peppercorn."

No group of the human race is homogeneous in color of skin or color and texture of hair. However, black, coarse, kinky, curly or wooly hair is mostly associated with blacks, and wavy hair is associated with whites, while black and straight hair is common among Orientals.

That classification is not entirely true. Some blacks have wavy and straight hair, as well as sandy colors and brown-black. Many whites have straight or coarse hair. In fact, some blonds have kinky or curly hair. Although most Orientals have thick and strong black hair, wavy and kinky are not uncommon among them. The Dravidians of India have wavy hair.

The Chinese usually have black hair, yet a great number have light brown or brunette hair. There are also those who have a tinge of red to their hair.

Kenneth Scott Latourette has this to say about the Chinese's head hair: "Chinese are usually black of hair, yet many, especially among the children, have light-brown hair, and a reddish tinge is not unknown." [1]

In fact, ancient Chinese writings or inscriptions mentioned blonds among their people. Many indigenous northern Koreans have blond hair and blue eyes.

A variety of hair texture is found among people all over the world, especially among South Pacific Islanders of Melanesia, Polynesia and Micronesia. It may interest you to know that more than one texture of hair is found on a single head! For example, there are between 90,000 and 140,000 strands of hair on just one head. Among these numbers, different textures—wavy, straight, curly or kinky—may exist. However, one texture usually dominates. Other varieties may be so insignificantly small that they can hardly be felt or noticed.

Why, though, is a particular kind of color and texture of hair common among a color group?

CLIMATE AND DIFFERENCES IN HAIR

Take a quick trip around the world in your mind. What do you find about color and texture of hair? That the colder the climate, the more variety there is in colors of hair, and the hairs are either wavy or straight. On the other hand, the hotter the climate, the darker and curlier the hair. Between tropical and temperate climates is the monsoon type of climate found in most of Asia. So most Asians have black and straight hair—a type of hair that is between blacks' and whites' hair.

An exception to the rule of cold climate and more variety of hair are the Eskimos. Because the Eskimos originated from Asia, they had developed their color and texture of hair before they migrated to North America.

The great majority of native Africans, Asians, South and Central Americans have black hair. Black hair also dominates the islands of the Pacific and the Atlantic. In southern Europe where it is warm, most people have black hair. The countries of southern Europe where black hair predominates include Greece, Spain, Portugal, Malta and Albania.

A desert climate is no hotter than a tropical climate. In both climates, temperature hovers around 100°F in the summer. Native desert dwellers, such as the Pygmies of the Kalahari in Africa, have spiralled or "peppercorn" kind of hair. That kind of hair seems more coarse in texture than hair type prevailing in the rest of black Africa.

In the same country, colors of hair differ under different climatic conditions. For example, southern Italians, such as the

Sicilians who live in a subtropical climate, have predominantly black hair. On the other hand, northern Italians who live in a colder climate than the Southerners abound in blond, red, and brunette colors. And the incidence of red, blond, and brunette hair are common in northern Europe which is colder than southern Europe.

Evidently, what we have discussed about skin pigmentation and climate applies with equal force to the color of head hair. As the climate pigments the skin, so it does head hair through the same process of body chemical reactions we discussed earlier. The body chemicals work in orchestration to pigment, not only the skin, the head hair, but, as we will discuss, also the eyes.

SUITABILITY OF HAIR FOR CLIMATE

The different kinds of hair found among different color groups is *best suited* for the climate under which they live. For example, black and "kinky" or wooly hair is best suited for the hot climatic conditions, say, of Africa and other parts of the world, whereas wavy hair is best suited for cold conditions. Wooly or kinky hair can withstand heat better than other colors or textures, especially wavy hair.

In fact, under the burning heat of the sun, accompanied by humidity or sweat, wavy hair, typical of whites, looks as if it has just been washed or becomes withered. That does not happen to black and wooly hair, for it maintains its texture all the time.

On the other hand, wavy hair is good for protection against cold conditions because it traps air. The trapped air acts as an *insulator* to keep the head warm in much the same way as the fur on a polar bear traps air to insulate the bear from the frigid arctic and subarctic climates.

Black or wooly hair, typical of blacks, cannot trap air, so it is constantly bathed with cold air if the black person lives in a cold climate and does not wear a head covering. Because it lacks the inherent ability to trap air, the kinky or curly hair, if not well cared for, becomes brittle and breaks easily in cold climates. The scalp may also suffer.

It is a blessing that the black and kinky hair does not have insulating ability, for that would mean that the hair would trap water and heat. If it did *and at the same time maintained its texture*, it would make the head unbearably warm. Physical activities would be very uncomfortable and greatly curtailed, thereby making the margin of survival dangerously narrow.

The fact that wavy hair gets wet when one works in the heat is also a blessing, because the sweat easily absorbed into the hair acts to cool the head. If wavy hair absorbed heat and at the same time maintained its texture, the head would become unbearably warm and thus make survival hang in the balance in hot weather.

The body maintains a constant temperature of 98.6°. That kind of temperature, combined with 80 to 100°F heat produced by the sun, can cause the blood to boil. But, fortunately, the body has a built-in "thermostat" or heat regulator. However, if wavy hair retained water, the combined temperature of the body and the sun could make the trapped water in the hair boil. But, as noted, neither curly nor wavy hair can trap water.

Black and straight hair is most suited for the climate under which it is found, which is mostly in Asia. This type of hair is between the characteristics of hair of whites and blacks, much the same way as the colors of people living in Asia and the climate under which they live is between the extremes of cold and hot. Oriental hair has some measure of insulating power, but not to the degree that wavy hair has. Consequently, Oriental hair does not get wet quickly under physical exertion in a hot condition as wavy hair does. At the same time, it does not remain unyielding, when wet, as does wooly or "kinky" hair.

HAIR PLIABILITY

Wavy and straight hair are much easier to comb than black and curly hair. Why?

For one thing, wavy and straight hair is porous; it can absorb water or other liquids, which is why it loses its texture or staying power when wet. However, the curly or kinky hair cannot absorb liquid, which is why it always maintains its texture, whether washed or not.

Curly hair is also difficult to comb because it twists and tangles as it grows. It grows in, whereas straight and wavy hair grows out. Curly or kinky hair may not be cut for months and will still not look long. (But it will look dense.) On the other hand, straight and wavy hair will grow long, or out, within a few months of having been cut.

There is another important reason why curly hair is not too pliable. You will recall that we mentioned in the last chapter that sebaceous glands produce oil. The root (follicle) of each hair contains a sebaceous gland which acts as a lubricant to the hair. Since wavy and straight hairs can absorb fluids, they are lubricated by the sebaceous glands. That is an additional, and perhaps the most important, reason why they are easy to comb. But the oil produced in the roots of curly hair, while it can nourish the hair's roots, cannot be absorbed by the hair, thus making curly hair difficult to comb. Hence it breaks under the pressure applied by a comb.

But what usually happens to the oil produced by sebaceous glands if one has curly hair? You may have noticed that the forehead of a person with curly hair usually looks oily. The oil that the sebaceous glands produce (and additional introduced oil) that cannot be absorbed by the hair is what moistens the forehead. That is also why the shirt collar of a black person may become dirty more quickly than the collar of a white person. We should also recall that dark-skinned people have more sweat glands than fair-skinned people, and that the forehead is among the parts of the body more copiously endowed with sweat glands.

A bald person's head usually looks shiny or somewhat glossy if the sebaceous glands in the bald areas are still active.

Since our discussion has shown climate to be the factor that determines the color and texture of hair, it stands to reason that if the ancestors of those who have red, blond and brunette types of hair had settled in hot climates, their hair would be dominantly black and curly. On the other hand, if the ancestors of those with dominantly black hair had settled in cold climates, they would have a variety of hair colors, as do present cold climatic dwellers.

To further support the statement made in the previous paragraph, let us use the white skin group of the human family as an example. Have you ever noticed that those with black hair usually have marginally darker skin than those with brunette hair, and those with brunette hair are normally marginally darker of skin than blonds, and blonds have marginally darker skin color than those with red hair? While there are exceptions to the rule of color of hair and degree of skin pigmentation, the rule shows that the hair and the skin are pigmented consecutively with melanin. Also, because of the variations in the amount of melanin in the skin, some get tanned more quickly than others.

HAIR AND AUSTRALIAN ABORIGINES

Our discussion of colors and textures of hair will prove incomplete if we fail to touch on the Aborigines of Australia. Needless to say, they are black and many of them have black hair, but there are also brunette, blond and other colors of hair. These types of hair are thick and stronger-looking than European blonds and brunettes. The Aborigines' hair textures include wavy, straight and coarse or kinky.

How do we explain these kinds of hair peculiar to Australian Aborigines? The Aborigines' case is an exceptional one, even more so because not all Aborigines have blond or brunette and wavy kinds of hair. The fact that man cannot explain why some of the Aborigines of Australia have these kinds of hair shows that man still has a lot to learn about himself and, indeed, about such simple things as the hair on his head. Also, the Australian Aborigines' types of hair demonstrate that all humans have common origin and these varieties exist within that one stock.

Like pigmentation, hair color does not change overnight. That is why the Eskimos, although living in a very cold climate, still have the same hair color that they developed in Asia. That is also why blacks who live in cold climates have not developed different colors and textures of hair. And that is why Southern Italians, Spanish, Portuguese, Maltese and others who live in the cold climates of either Europe or North America have not changed their black hair to other colors, such as blond or red. Hair color or pigmentation will hardly change sooner than skin pigmentation. They will probably both change gradually and concurrently through climatic interaction.

As can be seen, color or texture of hair does not make people superior or inferior. Rather, each person should be grateful for the type of hair (if he has any left) he has. As in all other things, variety in head hair should be welcomed.

BODY HAIR

People with white skin usually have more body hair than blacks or Orientals.

What determines body hair? Genes, of course, but climate plays a role, too. How so? Well, again, the colder the climate, the more profuse body hair usually is. The warmer the climate, the scantier body hair seems to be. It appears, therefore, that *cold climate activates the body to produce more hair for warmth.*

True, humans do not depend on body hair, as do animals, for warmth, yet it seems more than sheer coincidence that people living in cold climates have more body hair than people living in hot climates. Differences in the amount of body hair can be noted among people living even in the same country, but under different climatic variations. Take India as an example. Indians living in the north, which is relatively cold, generally have more body hair than dark people living in southern India where the prevailing climate is tropical.

The Ainu who live in the northernmost parts of Japan are another example. They are sometimes referred to as "Hairy Ainu" because they have more body hair than the typical Oriental. What is the origin of the Ainu?

"Scientists are uncertain about the origin of the Ainu," says

The World Book Encyclopedia. "Some scientists think they are related to European peoples. Other anthropologists believe they are related to Asian peoples or Australian Aborigines, the original inhabitants of Australia." [2]

If the Ainu are related to the Asians or the Aborigines, why is it that they have more body hair than those people? And if they are truly related to the Europeans, why is it that the Ainu do not have as much body hair as the typical European? Regardless of whom the Ainu are related to, they appear to be unique. Is it not consistent with our line of reasoning to conclude that the Ainu's body hair was precipitated by the severe and long winters of northern Japan?

ANIMALS AND FUR

Animals living in cold climates usually have thicker fur than their counterparts living in warm or hot regions. The bear is an example. Bears living in temperate regions have thicker wool than those living in warm climates. Polar bears have thicker fur than any other species of bear.

Also, birds living in arctic and subarctic climates have fuller plumage than those living in warmer climates. The owl is a case in point. Of the 525 species of owls, the Snowy Owl, which lives in arctic and subarctic climates, has feathers which are far better developed than those of the rest of the owl species. The claws and beaks of arctic and subarctic owls are almost completely covered with feathers, while the other owl species are not so prodigiously feathered. That is especially true of the burrowing owl, which exists in a protective underground dwelling and appears to be more scantily feathered than other owl species. Climate seems to be the only concrete reason for the differences in the richness of the owl species' plumage.

EYES

Colors of the eyes include brown, black, yellow, blue, green or hazel. (In filling a form, a person said that the color of his eyes to be "red.") These eye colors are found among people with all colors of skin. Although epicanthic eyes are common among Orientals, not all Orientals have epicanthic eyes.

Latourette says:, "Chinese are usually spoken of as 'slanted-eyed,' yet great numbers entirely lack that kind of physiognomy." [3] Though not common, relatively few blacks and whites have epicanthic eyes.

As with the skin and the hair, the color of the eyes is also determined by the amount of melanin in the body. It is believed that *most* humans have enough melanin in their eyes to give the iris brown pigmentation. The more pigmented the eyes, the less sensitive they are to the sun, which is why most dark-skinned people are less sensitive to sunlight. As a general rule, the darker the skin, the darker the iris. So the sun which precipitates the pigmentation of the skin also triggers the pigmentation of the eye.

Northern Europeans have a high incidence of blue, green or hazel eyes. In southern Europe, brown eyes are common. Northern Italians often have blue eyes while southern Italians have dark eyes. Some northern Chinese have blue eyes, but the southern dwellers have dark eyes. Relatively few blacks have blue or green eyes.

Nose

Take a deep breath! How do you feel? Fine? If so, we are now ready to tackle our next subject—the nose.

As we all know, most whites have rather pointed noses with narrow nostrils, although there are a few who have flat noses. A good many have medium-sized noses. The Middle Easterners generally have the same type of noses as whites, but with some variations. Most blacks, Far Easterners and Islanders have flat noses with a wider nasal index than whites. However, there are blacks as well as Orientals who have pointed noses identical to those of Europeans. Of course, there are other infinite varieties of shapes and sizes. Needless to say, none of the types of noses mentioned proves superiority or inferiority as far as breathing is concerned. What, however, accounts for the differences in the size and shape?

Scientists are unsure about the reasons for variations in shapes and sizes of noses. Theories advanced include such things as "mutant genes," "genetic drift," "natural or social selection." It has also been said that a long and narrow nose and nostril, generally typical of whites, makes breathing more efficient at relatively low temperatures, whereas short and flat noses, such as those typical of blacks and Orientals, function better at high temperatures. In other words, in hot climates the need to inhale oxygen due to heat is greater than in cold climates, implying the need for broader and shorter noses. That sounds logical and credible. This may be one of the reasons why a white person usually functions better in cold climates than a black person, and vice versa. However, our original question as to the *cause* of different sizes and shapes of noses remains to be answered.

Let us take a moment to discuss why "mutant genes," "genetic drift," and "natural and social selection" can hardly be the reasons behind the variations in noses.

Mutant Genes

Mutation in genes is usually detrimental to the organism in which it occurs. It is an indication that something has gone wrong in the molecular mechanism. In fact, mutation is a genetic accident which, like any other accident, does not usually benefit its victim.

Organic matter does not often experience "accidents" like inorganic things or man-made machines do, hence, it is appropriate to consider what scientists have to say about gene mutation or genetic accidents.

Professor John W. Klotz says: "The chemical nature of DNA [deoxyribonucleic acid] restricts the direction of mutation in that only certain bodies or breaks can be made in a complex biological compound without destroying it." [4]

Professor T. Dobzhansky of Columbia University says: "Mutational changes in any one gene are rare events. This is a different way of saying, ordinarily, the genes reproduce themselves accurately." [5]

It is obvious from those quotes that mutation in genes, the molecular machine of life, is very rare, and when it occurs, it is often destructive. How destructive gene mutation could be is forcefully put by *Encyclopedia Americana* (Vol. 10, 1982): "A majority of newly arisen mutants [mutated or altered genes] are deleterious [destructive] to their carriers. As stated above, mutations form a spectrum, ranging from changes so drastic that they cause death [or] lethal hereditary diseases . . . *The fact that most mutations are damaging to the organism seems hard to reconcile with the view that mutation is the source of raw materials for evolution.* Indeed, mutants illustrated in biology textbooks are a collection of freaks and monstrosities and mutation seems to be destructive rather than a constructive process. (Italics ours).

Some scientists say that about one percent of mutations could be beneficial. What, then, is the chance of cumulative beneficial mutation occurring? That, in the opinion of Professor J. Huxley, is highly unlikely:

We should clearly have to breed a thousand strains to get one with favorable mutations; a million strains (a thousand squared) to get one containing two favorable mutations; and so on, up to a thousand to the millionth power to get one containing a million. . . . A thousand to the millionth power, when written out, becomes the figure 1 with three million zeros after it: and that would take three large volumes of about five hundred pages each, just to print! Actually this is a meaninglessly large figure, but it shows what a degree of improbability natural selection has to surmount, and can circumvent. One with three million zeros after it is the measure of unlikeliness.[6]

Professor Gaylord Simpson said: Simultaneous appearance of several gene mutations in one individual has never been observed, so far as I know, and any theoretical assertion that this is an important factor in evolution can be dismissed. Even throughout the vast span of geological time the probability of such an event is negligibly small. For instance, postulating a mutation rate of .00001 and supposing that the occurrence of each mutation doubled the chances of another mutation in the same cell—a greater departure from random incidence than is likely to occur—the probability that five simultaneous mutations would occur in any one individual would be about .000000000000000000001. In an average population of 100,000,000 individuals with an average length of generation of only one day, such an event could be expected only once in about 274,000,000,000 years.[7]

The known universe is believed to be only 15,000,000,000 years old. The earth is said to be about 5,000,000,000 years old. Hence it appears that the universe is not old enough for that kind of mutation to occur.

Genetic Drift

Genetic drift is like genetic mutation or genetic accident. The arguments we presented about mutant genes apply here in full force, for genetic drift is more or less like mutant genes.

If "mutant genes," or "genetic drift," are not the causes of variations in nose, why, then, are flat noses common among most Africans and Orientals, while the high-bridged and pointed types of noses are prevalent among Europeans?

CLIMATE AND NOSES

To pinpoint the seeming reason for nose differences we need to zero in on two things together: noses and skin color. Since noses generally get progressively shorter and flatter as the climate gets progressively warmer and the skin gets gradually darker, and since noses get progressively longer and narrowed as the climate gets progressively colder and the skin becomes generally lighter, it would seem that the genes which control the skin and the nose have interacted over the years on different groups of people. The interaction may very well have been triggered by climatic factors in much the same way as skin pigmentation is controlled by climate. (Also, where a black or a yellow person has the long and high-bridged nose typical of a white person, the nasal index is usually wider.) That seems to be the crux of differences in noses among color groups living under different climatic conditions.

Here again, many southern Europeans do not have noses as high-bridged as those of northern Europeans. The Ainus (mentioned earlier) have the same high incidence of pointed noses typical of Europeans; yet, except for physical features which are strikingly similar, the Ainu's language and culture are completely unrelated to the Europeans. But northern Japan is colder than southern Europe.

In northern India where the climate is cold, most people have fair skin and pointed noses. In southern India where the climate is hot, the incidence of black skin and flat noses is great.

WHITES, HOT CLIMATES AND FLAT NOSES

If climate truly plays a major role in the shape of the noses and nasal index, why have not whites living in hot climates, such as in Africa or Australia, developed flat noses?

It seems skin pigmentation and the development of flat noses are inseparable. It is, therefore, not to be expected that whites living in hot climates would develop flat noses without also developing skin pigmentation.

Further, as we have noted, the Industrial and Agricultural Revolutions had already taken place before whites migrated in great numbers to the hot climatic regions of the world, so that the need for them to labor in the sun, which precipitates skin pigmentation and probably flatness of the nose, was not great at any time.

THE ESKIMOS AND NOSES

If cold climate plays a part in the incidence of high-bridged and narrow noses, and hot climate plays a role in the development of flat noses, one might reason that the Eskimos living in subarctic and arctic climatic conditions should have noses more high-bridged and pointed than the Europeans. Why are they not so endowed.

The Eskimos developed their shape of nose and other physical features before migrating to the subarctic and arctic regions of the world. Of course, some Eskimos have pointed noses, as do some of their counterparts in Asia, and blacks as well.

EVOLUTION AND TYPES OF NOSES

If sizes and shapes of noses are truly determined by the interaction of climatic variations on genes, is that not evolutionary? No. Humans have many latent built-in abilities to survive. Many of the built-in abilities are never used in a lifetime if circumstances or environmental factors do not trigger them. The production of skin pigmentation is a strong example. As we have noted, all humans (except albinos) have the potential to turn black, yet the majority of humans are not black.

Furthermore, organic evolution basically has to do with the progressive development of new and better body organs. People have always breathed with their noses, and there is no known record of people who have perished because of their inability to evolve more efficient noses. Moreover, sizes and shapes of noses are never homogeneous among people of the same color or living under the same climatic conditions. Also, no one has developed a supernose that can breathe better than other shapes and sizes of noses. Evolution has not given birth to, for example, a nose with three nasal indexes, or one with a superhole like a pipeline. Can we conclude, then, that the shapes and sizes of noses found among people today are due to evolutionary development? Or that the distinct differences in nose structures portray a picture of inferiority or superiority of race?

Are you breathing? We certainly hope so. So let us breeze to our next subject.

NOTES

1. Kenneth Scott Latourette, *The Chinese, Their History and Culture,* (New York, Macmillan, 1934), p. 3.

2. *The World Book Encyclopedia,* Vol. 1, (Chicago, World Book Inc., 1984), p. 153.

3. Latourette, p. 3.

4. John W. Klotz, *Genes, Genesis and Evolution,* (St. Louis, Concordia, 1972), p. 285.

5. T. Dobzhansky, *Radiation, Genes and Man,* (New York, Holt, Rinehart and Winston, 1959), p. 35.

6. J. Huxley, *Evolution in Action,* (New York, Harper and Row, 1953), p. 46.

7. Gaylord Simpson, *Mode in Evolution,* (New York, Hafner, 1965), pp. 54-55.

FIVE

SONS OF NOAH, BLACK PEOPLE
AND THE REST OF US

The three sons of Noah were Shem, Ham and Japheth and Ham was the forefather of the inhabitants of Africa. The name Ham means "swarthy, sunburnt, hot." The Bible says that Ham was the father of Canaan: "The sons of Noah who came out of the ark were Shem, Ham and Japheth; Ham was the father of Canaan" (Gen. 9:18). In addition to Canaan, Ham had other sons: "Cush, Mizraim [and] Put" (Gen. 10:6).

All respected Biblical and secular authorities agree that Africa was settled by Cush. The name Cushite is synonymous with Ethiopia. *Encyclopedia Americana,* confirming the fact that Cush settled in Africa says: "Cush was also called Kush, Nubia, and Ethiopia."

Are we to conclude then that the black people of Africa and other parts of the world were all descendants of Cush and perhaps also Put, and that their skin was black from the beginning, especially since Ham's name means "swarthy, sunburnt, hot"? No, not at all. For the reasons already presented in Chapter 3, the skin of some descendants of Adam and Eve could hardly be dark at the beginning while the skin of others remained light. Also, it is inconceivable to think that the skin of some of the global flood survivors changed color immediately following the flood. It can be convincingly proven that the skin color of people, especially of Ham's sons, was not black from the very beginning.

OTHER SONS OF HAM AND COLOR OF SKIN

According to Genesis, Ham's second son, Mizraim, was the forefather of the Philistines, and yet the Philistines were not black.

About Mizraim we read: "From Mizraim sprang the Lydians, Anamites, Lehabites, Naphtuhites, Pathrusites, Casluhites, and the Caphtorites, from whom the Philistines were descended" (Gen. 10:13-14). Canaan, also a son of Ham, is another example: "Canaan was the father of Sidon, who was his eldest son, and Heth" (Gen. 10:15).

The Canaanites settled in Sidon, which is part of modern Palestine. The land of Canaan also included the modern day Israel before the Israelites dispossessed the Canaanites of the land that was "flowing with milk and honey."

Encyclopedia Americana (Vol. 5, 1986) says: "Canaan was the name later called Palestine. Its original inhabitants were called Canaanites. The names occur in Cuneiform, Egyptian, and Phoenician sources from the 15th century B.C. on, and in the Bible."

The name Jerusalem originated from the word Jebusite, which was the name of a descendent of Canaan: "Canaan was the father of Sidon . . . and Heth, the Jebusites, the Amorites, the Girgashites" (Gen. 10:15-16). We do not need to be reminded that the non-Semitic Palestinians are not black—Palestinians who are black are probably descendants of the Africans taken by the Arabs during the slave trade—yet they are descendants of Ham. Ham was the father of Cush, yet Cush's descendants, the Ethiopians, are black. Are you surprised? You shouldn't be, especially in view of our discussion in a previous chapter about colors of skin.

It seems appropriate here, if we are to establish beyond any doubt the color of skin of the sons of Noah and their children and grandchildren, that we step back in time and examine the skin colors of people living before Noah's flood. Our examination will take us back once again to the starting point of man—the creation of Adam and Eve.

ADAM AND EVE

The Bible says that we are all offspring of Adam and Eve, and science has proved (as discussed in Chapter 2) beyond any doubt that mankind is from only one stock. The name Adam means "earthling man, mankind" and it is from the root word meaning "red" or "ruddy." And, according to Genesis, Eve was taken from Adam.

A MAN WITH A WOMB!

Let us consider briefly the biological or physiological closeness of man and woman. The Hebrew word for man is *ish*, and for woman is *ish-sha*. Ish-sha means female man, or a man with a womb, wombman. From this we have the word woman—a man with a womb. Its Greek equivalent is *gyne*, which means woman or wife. Apart from sizes of bustline, genital differences and the absence of a womb in man, there are other physical characteristics which show that the woman is from the man. For example, a man can produce milk much the same as a woman can, especially if the man's nipples are activated by being consistently suckled over a period of time. Some women, on the other hand, do grow a scanty beard or mustache. Many women have a profusion of arm hair, pelvic hair and sparse chest hair.[1] These things are present among people all over the world. Therefore, Adam and Eve were an inseparable part of each other.

In view of the foregoing, Adam and Eve would, logically, be basically the same color. We can hardly expect the color of one to be radically different from that of the other as we have today. The color of the *first* human couple on earth should blend perfectly, especially since the bone used to create Eve was taken from Adam. And Adam could hardly be expected to have said that Eve was "bone of his bone and *flesh* of his flesh" if Eve's color was radically different from his.

A GLOBAL WARM CLIMATE

Another very important point to bear in mind is that before Noah's flood, the entire earth enjoyed a uniformity of climate that was probably tropical or subtropical. The climate was exquisitely warm and congenial to plant and animal life. Fossils of plants and animals associated with warm climates have been found in cold climatic regions of the world, including Antarctica. Freshly preserved remains of woolly mammoths have been found in Alaska and Siberia. Elephant, rhinoceros and other animal remains have also been discovered in Europe, Alaska, and Siberia. Remains of tropical plants, such as ferns, have been found in Alaska, Siberia and other cold climatic regions.

That the polar regions of the world once enjoyed a warm climate has been confirmed by many respected authorities, including Isaac Asimov. Regarding the presence of coal in Alaska, which indicates that Alaska once enjoyed a warm climate for a long time, Isaac Asimov says in his book, *The Ends of the Earth:*

> This showed that not only did forests once grow in Antarctica, but they must have done so luxuriously for over many years, since most of the coal deposits are thirteen feet thick. Where plant life exists, animal life does, too. There is

no exception to this rule on Earth today. We can assume, then, that in a plant-rich Antarctica, animals existed too.[2]

As explained in the Bible, there was a water canopy which enveloped or insulated the earth from the full glare of the sun's radiant energy before Noah's flood. In fact, the removal of this water canopy, which occurred as part of Noah's flood, caused the sudden and dramatic climatic change, to extremes of heat and cold that exist today.

Since the earth enjoyed a uniformity of climate before the flood, the effects of the sun on our terrestrial would generally be the same everywhere. Logically, then, the skin color of people living before the flood would generally be the same: "red" or "ruddy," the same as their parents, Adam and Eve. The antediluvians or people living before the deluge, could hardly have had the radically different colors of skin that there are today.

But what about post-diluvians? Now that the sun could penetrate the earth's atmosphere without any permanent obstruction or shield, did the color of skin of the post-diluvians change radically while they were all in the *same* location, namely, the Plains of Shinar in Mesopotamia or Babylon, where the Bible locates them? (Gen. 11:1-9).

Post-Diluvians And Color Of Skin

We have established that people living before the global deluge of Noah's day would basically have the same color of skin. It follows, then, that Noah and his wife, the forefather of the human family following the global cataclysm, would be of the same color. But what of Noah's offspring and descendants a few generations after the flood? These post-diluvians were living in the same location where they were united in building a tower or a ziggurat "whose top may reach unto heaven" (Gen. 11:4. King James). It was at this location where they were building the tower that God confused man's language (Gen. 11:4-9). It was also from this location that mankind scattered.

According to Bible chronology, from the end of the global deluge to the confusion of the language of the now rapidly multiplying offspring of Noah, 131 years passed. And since all the people living then *dwelt in the same location and under the same climatic condition*, their skin color should generally have been the same and not radically different from each other such as exists today.

Nonetheless, we are still faced with a seemingly formidable problem: The implication of the meaning of Ham's name. So let us see if we can untangle the paradox.

HAM—A NAME GIVEN AT BIRTH OR IN ADULT LIFE?

We have noted earlier in this chapter that Ham's name means "swarthy, sunburned, hot." It would have been utterly impossible for Ham to have become a "swarthy, sunburned, [or] hot" in his mother's womb so that when he was born he would be given the name Ham, describing his physical appearance. Rather, it seems highly likely that Ham developed, later in life, a sunburned complexion or a body whose temperature was raised by the sun or brisk activity in the sun to the point of profuse sweating. Hence the fitting name, Ham.

Like many other ancient people, Ham must have spent a large portion of his time outdoors, perhaps more so than his brothers. He must have worked in the field, which is why he could be "hot" or "sunburned." After all, farming or herding were about the main occupations available at the dawn of man's history. So Ham may have very well been given his name later in life to describe the effects his outdoor activities had upon him. In the past, people were given names describing their occupations, such as Smith (from blacksmith), Carpenter (describing his occupation of working with wood), Cooper (describing a coppersmith), and so forth. Jesus was called "the carpenter's son."

This does not mean that Ham's brothers were not sunburned, but it is not logical or practical to think that all the three sons of Noah (perhaps their wives, too) would be given a name showing that they were sunburned. In any event, babies are not born black or sunburned. Is there any reason to believe that Ham would have been an exception? Furthermore, the name Ethiopia is a Greek word which means "region of sunburned faces," which makes it all the more likely that Ham must have been given his name as a result of how the sun affected his skin.

HAM—A NAME GIVEN AT BIRTH?

Although highly unlikely, let us assume that Ham was given his name at birth. How, then, do we account for such a name?

Ham must have been of the same color as his brothers, but he may have had a *slightly darker variation of the same color. And all whites are not exactly the same shade and all blacks are not exactly the same shade,* yet that does not discount the fact that they are either blacks or whites. This variation of shade occurs even among children of the *same parents of the same color of skin,* whether of white, black or yellow parents.

Look at it this way: Would you expect a white couple to have *completely* black or "ebony-black" children? Would you expect a clear black couple to have children who are white, blond (or red-head) with blue eyes and wavy hair? That seems ordinarily impossible. Well, if we are to believe that Ham was black at the beginning that is how we would expect his children to turn out. We would expect such phenomena to occur, not only in Ham, but also in both Noah and his wife and in Adam and Eve, for they were the grandparents of us all—if you believe in the Bible.

There seems hardly any doubt, then, that *all* of Noah's sons and Ham's sons must have been of the same color of skin when they were born, though shades may have been marginally varied. Only later on did the pigmentation that was part of Adam's make-up, and that Noah inherited from Adam and that we, in turn, inherited from Noah, developed according to the degree that the skin was exposed to the sun. So over the millenniums the sun had activated the melanin in the bodies of many and thus resulted in dark skin color—dark enough for the Bible to refer to it about 1,800 years after Noah's flood, "Can the Ethiopian [3] change his skin, or the leopard his spots?" (Jer. 13:23. KJ).

The statement in Jeremiah was not uttered for derogatory or discriminatory reasons as may be done today. Rather, it was used illustratively to point to the depth of spiritual decadence of the sons of Israel. The skin is more than a mere surface affair, as we have seen in Chapter Three. Just as the moral decay of the sons of Israel was deep, skin pigmentation is more than superficial. Otherwise, one would be able to wash or scrub it off easily, just as the seven-year-old girl in the entrance of First Baptist Church was so determined to do.

In passing it might be said that at the inception of man, before climate pigmented the skin, people would not be described by color. Also, before the Europeans discovered the black people, it does not seem that there would have been any reason for the Europeans to describe a person by color of skin. It also seems there would have been no need for the black and yellow members of the human family to describe others by color before they encountered other colors. So, after encountering each other for the first time, the white man would say he saw a black or a yellow man, the black or yellow man would say he saw a white man. The point we are getting at here is that climatic factors are the reason for describing people according to the color of their skin. The same rule could be applied to Ham: he was called swarthy or sun-burned only after climate had interacted with his inherent ability for his skin to pigment.

WATER CANOPY AND THE SUN

Before Noah's flood, we have noted that a water canopy shielded the earth. For that reason, the radiant energy of the sun was not felt on the earth then as it is felt today. That brings up a question: Could the sun have penetrated the canopy to the extent that one could be hot or sunburned? Yes! Otherwise how could Ham (and perhaps others) have been sunburned? Also, the whole earth enjoyed an exquisite warm climate before Noah's flood. More importantly, the process of photosynthesis, whereby plants utilize the sun's energy for growth, would have been impossible without the radiant energy of the sun. If the sun penetrates the azure blue Caribbean ocean, why would the sun have been unable to penetrate the water canopy before Noah's flood?

But since pigmentation of the skin is an extremely slow process, would Ham have lived a lifespan long enough to allow his skin to be, not black, but noticeably pigmented?

NOAH'S FAMILY

If Ham was swarthy or sunburned, which is the focus of all evidence so far on that point, he must have spent a considerable amount of time in the sun in order for him to be *marginally* dark in comparison to his brothers.

How do we know that Ham must have exposed himself to the sun for a long time? First of all, we do not know how old Noah was when he married, but we know how old he was when he had his three sons: "Noah was five hundred years when he begot Shem, Ham and Japhet" (Gen. 5:32). But the deluge did not occur until the six hundredth year of Noah's life, for we are informed: "In the year when Noah was six hundred years old, on the seventeenth day of the second month, on that very day, all the springs of the great abyss broke through, the windows of the sky were opened, and rain fell on the earth for forty days and forty nights" (Gen. 10:11).

Since the flood occurred in the six hundredth year of Noah's life, and Noah started to father children when he was 500 years old, and Shem was 100 years old two years after the flood, (Gen. 11:10), it follows that his younger brother, Ham, would have been close to that age also. Even if we assume a difference of six years between the birth of Shem and Ham, Ham would still be at least 90 years old after the flood.

Therefore, Ham had several decades of opportunity to expose himself to the sun so as to warrant being given a name that means "swarthy," "hot," or "sunburned."

It is also possible that Ham was given his name *after* the flood, since it is not unusual in Bible times, and even nowadays, to be given a name in adult life by which thereafter one is popularly known. *Aid to Bible Understanding* says: "At times new names were given to persons elevated to high governmental positions or to those to whom special privileges were extended. Since such names were bestowed by superiors, the name change might also signify that the bearer of the new name was subject to its giver." [4]

The book further explains: "An event in a person's later life sometimes provided the basis for giving a new name to a person. Esau (the brother of Jacob), for example, got his name Edom ("red, ruddy") from the *red* lentil stew for which he sold his birthright" (Genesis 25:30-34).[5]

There are, of course, several other examples that could be cited from the Bible where names of individuals were changed later in life. These include the name Abram ("father of exaltation") to Abraham ("father of multitude"), because he was to become the patriarchal father of the Hebrews and other nations (Genesis 17:5). Hence, the name Abraham was prophetic. The name of Abraham's wife was also changed from Sarai ("contentious") to Sarah ("princess") (Gen. 17:15, 16). That change of name also portrays, among other things, significant events in Sarah's life. Many of us hardly remember Abram or Sarai, but Abraham and Sarah readily come to mind. The name of Jacob was changed to Israel. Israel means "God contends" or "Contender with God," (Gen. 32:24-28), a result of Jacob's unyielding determination to wrest a blessing from a materialized angel.

From the foregoing, it seems that Ham may have had a given name later in life that stuck prominently more than his given name at birth.

Be that as it may, were any group of people destined to be of a particular color?

WHO WAS MEANT TO BE BLACK, WHITE OR YELLOW?

The fact that all people, regardless of color of skin, have within their bodies the potential to turn black shows that no one, at man's early beginning, was born or damned to be a particular color. If some people were originally meant to be either black, white or yellow, then there would be absolutely no need for all people to possess the inherent ability to turn either black or dark. If some people were originally meant to be either black, white or yellow, then the communality of origin of the human race, as scientifically, Biblically and logically established, would be open to serious doubts. But we ourselves are living and inescapable evidence that all humans came from one and only one source. We cannot deny that fact anymore than we can deny our own existence! Evidently, then, the endless varieties in colors of skin were a later phenomena that occurred sometime after the dispersal of humans from their very first settlement.

A FAMILY REMIXED

Cush was a son of Ham. Vitally important is the fact that Cush's wife's name, or the names of the wives of other grandsons of Noah, are not known; they are not mentioned in the Bible. Even the names of the wives of Noah's three sons and that of Noah's wife are not mentioned in the Bible, just as the names of the daughters of Eve and Adam are not recorded in the Bible.

Only one family survived the Noachian Flood. Undoubtedly, Cush, Put, or other grandsons and granddaughters of Noah married their brothers and sisters, nephews and nieces. As their population increased, marriages among the group would continue, thus resulting in the human race we have today. We do not want to forget that Abraham had an Egyptian concubine, Hagar, and also had Keturah as a concubine, or both of them as secondary wives. Hagar was from the line of Ham, and Keturah was probably from the line of Japheth.

It should be said that it was unlikely that only Cush and his wife and their children settled in Africa. It is not mentioned in the Bible that the grandsons and granddaughters of Noah mixed and settled in lands different from where their patriarchal fathers, the three sons of Noah, settled. That they all married into one another's families and settled in lands different from where their forefathers migrated was inevitable.

In his book, *The Language of the World,* Kenneth Katzner has this to say about Noah's offspring: "The terms Hamitic and Semitic are derived from the names of two of the [three] sons of Noah in the Bible, Ham and Shem. The undoubted kinship of their languages suggests that at one time they were one people, but if so it would have to have been prehistoric times. Perhaps one of those people migrated from the homeland of the other, but no one really knows." [6]

The *World Book Encyclopedia* says: "The Canaanites were a Semitic people, related to the Arabs, Assyrians, and the Israelites" (Volume 3, 1986). Although the Canaanites are said to be "Semitic people," the Canaanites' forefather is not Shem, as we have seen.

The Bible is quiet about this mixing because, in those days, God usually dealt with the oldest male member of the family. This arrangement is called patriarchal, where the father, or the oldest living male, is the ruler of the family. It is unnecessary for the Bible to list endless names since it has already stated in several places, such as Genesis 2:21-23; 3:20, Acts 17:25, that all humans are from one person, Adam. What is more, the Bible calls Noah's offspring "one people" (Gen. 11:6).

The Bible was not written for racial wranglings; there is only one human race as we have already noted.

MODERN EXAMPLES OF MIXTURE

We are all aware that the offspring of mixed black and white couples are called mulattoes. However, the children of mulattoes and whites are dubbed quadroon. Funk and Wagnalls *New Standard Dictionary*, 1963, defines quadroon as "a person having one-fourth negro and three-fourths white blood; the child of a mulatto and a white." But the offspring of white men and American Indian women, especially in South American countries, such as Brazil, are called "mamelucos." The offsprings of mulattoes and mamelucos are daubed "cafusos." French masters cohabited with black women. Their children are called creoles. While the negro males were mercilessly punished or killed for cohabiting with white women, "the sexual exploitation of negro women by white men continued to be tolerated," says *Encyclopedia Americana*, Volume 20, 1979.

The sexual exploitation and also marriages (in states where marriages between whites and blacks were legal) resulted in mixing and blending of colors. The *New Catholic Encyclopedia* confirms this: "Biologically, American Negroes represent a fusion of many African peoples and of white and American Indian strains as well. It is estimated that about 80 percent have some admixture of the latter strains [white and American Indian] received since the arrival of their ancestors in the New World."

To end this chapter and introduce the next, it might be appropriate to use the words of Isaac Asimov in his book, *Asimov's Guide to the Bible:* "Some moderns seem to think that Ham represents the Negro peoples and that this chapter [Genesis, Chapter 9, verse 25] can be used to justify Negro slavery. This is the purest piffle [rubbish, nonsense or trash]. Neither Ham, Canaan, nor any of their named descendants were viewed as Negroes by Biblical writers." [7]

If blacks were not cursed by God, and certainly not with color of skin or intelligence, who, then, was cursed and is the curse still potent?

NOTES

1. Hormone imbalance or malfunction, or drugs may produce in a female excessive hairs that are typical of a male.

2. Isaac Asimov, *The Ends of the Earth*, (New York, Weybright and Talley, 1975), p. 340.

3. Some Bible translations use the word "Cushite" instead of Ethiopian.

4. Watchtower Bible and Tract Society, *Aid to Bible Understanding*, New York, Watchtower, 1969), p. 1201.

5. Ibid., p. 1202.

6. Kenneth Katzner, *The Language of the World*, (New York, Funk & Wagnalls, 1975),   p. 30.

7. Isaac Asimov, *Asimov's Guide to the Bible*, (New York, Avenel Books, 1981), p. 45.

SIX

WHO WAS CURSED?

To quote once again from the Bible the circumstances that led to the curse:

> The sons of Noah who came out of the ark were Shem, Ham and Japheth; Ham was the father of Canaan. These three were the sons of Noah, and their descendants spread over the whole earth.
>
> Noah, a man of the soil, began the planting of vineyards. He drank some of the wine, became drunk and lay naked inside his tent. When Ham, the father of Canaan, saw his father naked, he told his two brothers outside. So Shem and Japheth took a cloak, put it on their shoulders and walked backwards, and so covered their father's naked body; their faces were turned the other way, so that they did not see their father naked. When Noah woke from his drunken sleep, he learnt what his youngest son had done to him, and said:
>
> > 'Cursed be Canaan,
> > slave of slaves
> > shall he be to his brothers' (Gen. 9:20-25).

"Cursed be Canaan," but who were the Canaanites? In addition to previous arguments, the land in which they settled proves that the Canaanites were not blacks.

Concerning their settlement, *Encyclopedia Americana* (Vol. 5, 1979) says: "The area referred to as Canaan in the early Egyptian sources extended along the entire eastern coast of the

Mediterranean Sea, from Tripoli (in present day Lebanon) in the north to Gaza in the south, and eastward to the Jordan River and the Dead Sea."

So Canaan, the forefather of the Palestinians, was the one cursed. (See map below.)

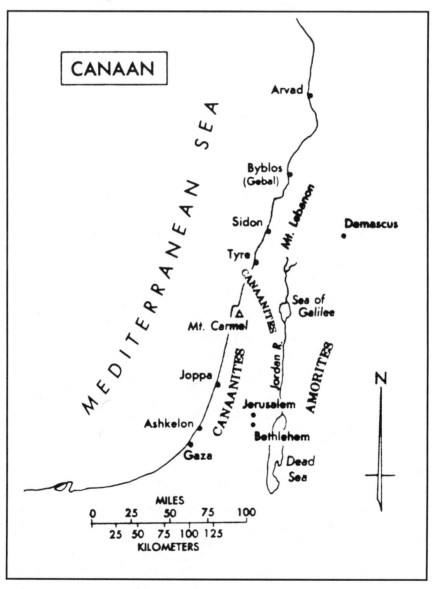

You may also have observed from the Bible quotation that Canaan was damned to be the servant of Shem or the Israelites. Has the curse been fulfilled? Yes.

The following quotes from the Bible support the fulfillment of the curse: "And they [Shemetic people or Israelites] did not drive away the Canaanites who were dwelling in Gezer, and the Canaanites continue dwelling in among Ephraim down to this day and came to be subject to slavish forced labor" (Joshua 16:10, New World Translation).

"And it turned out that when the sons of Israel had grown strong, they went putting the Canaanites at forced labor, and they did not dispossess them entirely" (Joshua 17:23, New World Translation).

"And it came about that Israel grew strong and proceeded to set the Canaanites to forced labor, and they did not drive them out completely. Neither did Ephraim drive out the Canaanites who were dwelling in Gezer, but the Canaanites continued to dwell among them in Gezer. Zebulun did not drive out the inhabitants of Kitron and the inhabitants of Nahalol, but the Canaanites continued to dwell in among them and came to be subject to forced labor" (Judges 1:28-30, N.W.T.).

In addition to being subjected "to forced labor" by the Israelites, the Canaanites were also later subjugated by Japheth's descendants, namely, Medo-Persia, Greece and Rome. *The curse has been fulfilled and it is no longer in force, even among the Palestinians.* Although the Middle Easterners do battle with each other, none of the Middle Eastern nations are subjected to another, either of the Middle East or others, nor are they enslaved because of a curse or for other reasons.

The *World Book Encyclopedia* (Vol. 3, 1980) has this to say about the Canaanites: "The Canaanites settled in Canaan, the Biblical name for Palestine, about 3000 B.C. They were chief inhabitants of this land until the Israelites conquered them about 1200 B.C." (Again, the land where the Canaanites settled showed that they were not black people, although offspring of Ham.)

Curse Doesn't Mention Intelligence

Certainly, the curse upon the Canaanites had nothing to do with their intelligence. The same *Encyclopedia* says: "Ancient remains show that the Canaanites had an advanced civilization."

Regarding them, *Encyclopedia Americana* (Vol. 21, 1979) says: "The Phoenician language holds the unique distinction of being the *first* to use exclusively and effectively an alphabet that was passed on to the Hebrews, Aramaenas, and Arabs, and to the

Greeks and the Romans." Therefore, the Phoenicians had played an indispensable part in the art of writing.

Moreover, the Canaanites had great military power, far stronger than that of the Israelites. It was only through divine backing, as explained in the Bible, that the Israelites, of inferior military strength, were able to subjugate and dispossess the Canaanites of their land—"a land flowing with milk and honey."

AFRICAN TECHNOLOGY AND KINGDOMS

So far we have proven that black people were not cursed by God, but even if they had been cursed, intelligence or natural ability had nothing to do with the curse. We will, however, consider briefly African technology and kingdoms, in further support of the fact the curse has nothing to do with black people or intelligence.

Concerning African technology, anthropologists have discovered that the Haya people of Tanzania were able to make carbon steel as far back as 2,000 years ago. This important discovery was made in the "West Lake" region of Tanzania, by anthropologist Peter Schmidt and Metallurgy Professor Donald Avery, both of Brown University. Commenting on this discovery, *Time* said:

> As long as 2,000 years ago, the Haya people were producing medium-carbon steel in preheated forced-draft furnaces. A technology this sophisticated was not developed again until nineteen centuries later, when German-born Metallurgist Karl Wilhelm Siemens, who is generally credited with using an open-hearth furnace, produced the first high-grade carbon steel.[1]

Of course, what the scientists "found was beyond their expectation." Further commenting on the impact of the discovery the magazine *Science* said:

> One of the more profound implications of the West Lake discoveries is that we are now able to say a technologically superior iron-smelting process developed in Africa more than 1,500 years ago. This knowledge will help to change scholarly and popular ideas that technological sophistication developed in Europe but not in Africa.[2]

Several kingdoms and empires flourished in Africa for centuries. These included the West African kingdoms of Kanem-Bornu, Ife and Benin, all in Nigeria. There were also those of the Ashanti of Ghana, of Timbuktu in Mali, in which colleges of advanced learning had been in operation since the Middle Ages.

The Songhai empire replaced that of Mali. There were also the Agadez, Gao and the Mossi states Kingdoms. South and Central African kingdoms include those of Kongo of the Luba people (now Zaire), and the kingdom of Karanga people (or Mwanamutapa), which is the present day Zimbabwe (formerly Rhodesia). In ancient times, the capital of the kingdom of Karanga people was the Great Zimbabwe.

One may, however, reason, "The underdeveloped people were very clever in those days, but I am not sure of the modern generations. If they are as smart as their ancestors, why can't they help themselves?"

The reasons for the apparent inability of underdeveloped people to help themselves is not subject of our discussion, yet we can say that in view of our discussion in Chapter Two, some cultures failed to advance scientifically and technologically not because of inherent inferior mental ability, but due to interwoven external factors.

Quite fittingly, then, Professors Boyd and Asimov could say about intelligence: "Certainly, though, it can be said that, whatever gene that controls intelligence and various kinds of talent, no one race [or color of skin, language, culture, etc.] has a monopoly, or even a lion's share, of them. People with all sorts of talents are produced by all races."[3]

Moreover, close examination of the anatomical makeup of the brains of different color or ethnic groups has not revealed any differences, though variation in size exists within *all* color groups.

Take as an example the words of Professor W.E. Le Gros Clark, an outstanding anthropologist and physical anatomist of Oxford University in England. Professor Clark has been described as "one of the most distinguished neuro-anatomists . . . of the day." He says: "In spite of statements which have been made to the contrary, there is no macroscopic [large enough to be seen or observed by the naked eye] or microscopic difference by which it is possible for the anatomist to distinguish the brains of individuals of different races." [4]

You may have noticed that, although Ham was the one who "saw his father naked," yet Canaan, a son of Ham, was the one cursed. Is it not an act of injustice for the son to suffer for the sin of his father?

THE SINS OF FATHERS ON THEIR OFFSPRING—AN INJUSTICE?

We requote Genesis: "When Ham, father of Canaan, saw his father naked, he told his brothers outside." Really, then, Canaan never saw the nakedness of Noah. Yet Noah said, in verse 25: "Cursed be Canaan, slave of slaves shall he be to his brothers."

Even more of an injustice is piled on if we also read Exodus 20:5. "Because I, Jehovah your God, am a God exacting exclusive devotion, bringing punishment for the error of fathers upon sons, upon third generation and upon the fourth generation, in the case of those who hated me" (N.W.T.). Basically, then, the Bible is saying that children to several generations would suffer for the sins of their parents.

Let it be realized, first of all, that God was dealing with the nation of Israel as an *entity* according to the book of Exodus we have just read. So these words of Exodus were addressed to the nation of Israel. Basically what God was telling the Israelites was that if they acted correctly they and their offsprings would live in peace. But if, on the other hand, they disobeyed God's law, the suffering that resulted from disobedience to God's clearly stated commands would *spread to, or affect* their children. It was a *community responsibility*. Let us illustrate this by the presence of pollution in the industrialized societies of today. Both those responsible for the pollution and those who are not suffer from it and die. Children, including those yet to be born, may suffer even though they did not cause the pollution or were even aware of how it was caused. It is a community or national ill that affects all. On the other hand, there is a Social Security or welfare system in many industrialized societies. Many who benefit from it do not know who organized it or when it was started. In fact, not only were they not even born when it was started, but their parents were not yet born, and many still to be born will benefit from it. That, too, is community or national responsibility. If a person enjoys the privileges of a society, he will also suffer penalties for the woes the society brings upon itself.

This is the same situation that existed between the nation of Israel and its Maker. If the Israelites disobeyed God, they and their children would suffer just as they did in 70 A.D. when both their city and temple were destroyed by the Romans. According to Jewish historian Flavius Josephus, 1,100,000 Israelites were destroyed and 97,000 were taken captive. On the other hand, when they obeyed God's law they benefited. During the reign of King Solomon, for instance, the Israelites enjoyed 40 years of peace, serenity and prosperity.

So it was with the Canaanites. God, being omnipotent and omniscient, foresaw the life pattern that the Canaanites would live, especially as exemplified by their forefather, Ham. Therefore, slavish labor was necessary to curb their recklessness, and the denunciation upon the Canaanites was not unwarranted since the Canaanites engaged in gross sexual sins: sex worship, orgies, adultery, temple prostitution, homosexuality and beastiality. They sacrificed children to their gods. Many of the children they let "pass through the fire" or burn alive in order to appease one of their fetish gods, Molech.

Warning the Israelites about the depravity of the Canaanites and other surrounding nations, the Bible says: "You shall not have sexual intercourse with the wife of your fellow-countryman and so make yourself unclean with her. You shall not surrender any of your children to Molech and thus profane the name of your God: I am the Lord. You shall not lie with a man as with a woman: that is an abomination. You shall not have sexual intercourse with any beast to make yourself unclean with it, nor shall a woman submit herself to intercourse with a beast; that is a violation of nature. You shall not make yourselves unclean in any of these ways; for in these ways the heathen, whom I am driving out before you, made themselves unclean. This is how the land became unclean, and I punished it for its iniquity so that it spewed out its inhabitants" (Lev. 18:20-25).

If you had a choice, would you want to live among such debased people? As a parent, would you allow somebody to burn your little boy or girl alive for the worship of a lifeless fetish god? Obviously then, it was absolutely necessary to stop such repulsive cruelty and promiscuity. Hence, under divine direction, the Israelites were able to conquer the Canaanites and dispossess them of their lands. Rather than a blatant injustice or an inhumane act, it was a display of love and justice on God's part.

To further show that God was not displaying favoritism on behalf of the Israelites and partiality against the Canaanites, the Bible addresses these words to the Israelites, the would-be conquerors of the Canaanites:

> When the Lord your God drives them out before you, do not say to yourselves, 'It is because of my own merit that the Lord has brought me in to occupy this land.' It is not because of your merit or your integrity that you are entering their land to occupy it; it is because of the wickedness of these nations that the Lord your God is driving them out before you, and to fulfill the promise which the Lord made to your forefather, Abraham, Isaac and Jacob. Know then that it is not because of any merit of yours that the Lord your God is giving you this rich land to occupy; indeed, you are a stubborn people. (Deut. 9:4-6).

In spite of community accountability, individuals who did what was right were approved by God: "It is the soul that sins, and no other, that shall die; a son shall not share a father's guilt, nor a father his son's. The righteous man shall reap the fruit of his own righteousness, and the wicked man the fruit of his own wickedness" (Eze. 18:20). After all, the dominant quality of God is love: "But exercising loving-kindness toward the thousandth generation[5] in the case of those who love me and keep my commandments" (Ex. 20:6, N.W.T.). The thousandth generation of loving kindness eclipses the "third" or "fourth generation" of punishment.

While it is quite obvious that the black people were not cursed, is there a pure or a "master race"? Some people contend, for their own purposes, that over a long period of time a new breed of "superior race" may have developed, in much the same way as people develop hardy types of crops or a particular breed of animal. In fact, many today preach the superiority of one color group over another.

NOTES

1. Peter Schmidt and Donald H. Avery, "Africa's Ancient Steelmakers," *Time*, Vol. 112, No. 13, 25 Sept. 1978, p. 80.

2. Peter Scmidt and Donald H. Avery, "Complex Iron Smelting and Prehistoric Culture in Tanzania," *Science*, Vol. 201, No. 4361, 22 Sept. 1978, p. 1085.

3. *Races and People*, p. 164.

4. W.E. Le Gros Clark, *Fitting Man to His Environment*, (New Castle, University of Newcastle upon Tyne, 1949), p. 19.

5. Although other versions say "thousands," the meaning is "generation." This is consistent with the context. See Deuteronomy 7:9 and Psalms 105:8.

SEVEN

Is There A Master Race?

"Herren Volk" or "Master Race," was the aspiration of Adolf Hitler regarding the Germans. He wanted no "contamination" of the Germans so that he could maintain the "racial purity" and thus make a "Master Race" out of them. Perhaps Hitler was unaware of the fact that Germany had been invaded several times in the past, especially between 1618 and 1815, by France, Sweden, England, Russia, Spain, Denmark, and Austria. During that period of invasions, the invaders interbred with the Germans.

Hitler himself may have been the result of "contamination" since he was not a German, but an Austrian. And, sure enough, throughout Austria's history, many different groups of people have settled in the country and intermixed. So the present-day population of Austria is a mixture of Celts, Romans, Germanic tribes, Hungarians, Slavs, Asians and others. As a result of this mixing, there is no "typical" Austrian. Some are fair-skinned and blond with blue eyes, others have dark skin, brown eyes, and brown hair. Yet Hitler's neurotic monomania was for a master race to rule Europe.

In order to promote his diabolic aspirations, Hitler destroyed about eleven million people, including six million Jews, and tortured countless others.

Hitler most likely thought that his obsession to create a thousand year "Third Reich" to be ruled by a "Master Race" was well underway after the conquest of Poland, the overrunning of most of Europe, and the fall of France to Germany in 1940. Hitler danced a joyous jig on the occasion of France's fall, but it was a dance of doom, for he died an inglorious death in late April of 1945 by committing suicide. The Jews live on. But where is Hitler today? Hitler and everything that was associated with his tyranny are now distasteful history, part of a cruel and bloody past.

But unfortunately, Hitler's psychosis lived on after his death. There are those who still believe in so-called "racial purity."

IN SEARCH OF "RACIAL PURITY" AROUND THE GLOBE

Let us engage in an imaginary trip around the world. To act as an impetus to our journey, we will arm ourselves with a few questions, such as: Were *only whites* the original inhabitants of Europe? Were *only blacks* the original inhabitants of Africa? Could it be that mixtures of blacks, whites, yellows and other shades were among the *indigenous* inhabitants of Europe, Africa, and other parts of the world? We may be in for a surprise. Let us start our journey in Africa.

Africa

The Moors, or the Berbers of northwest Africa, together with Arabs, invaded and conquered Spain in the early eighth Century of our Common Era and remained in parts of Spain for a period of nearly 800 years. During that long period of stay, the Berbers no doubt "interbred" with the Spaniards so that the Spaniards could rightly be said to have Moorish blood in them.

In the Somali Republic there are people with almond-shaped or epicanthic eyes. These people have thick and curly hair, instead of straight, as we find in the Orient. The people of Madagascar are believed to have migrated from the East Indies. They display "mixtures" of blacks, Indians, Arabs, Greeks and so forth. The people of Comoro Islands exhibit African, Arab, Malayan and European "extractions." The people of Mauritius have African, Indian, Chinese and other skin colors as original inhabitants. The Arabs took many African slaves. These have mixed with the Arabs in the same manner African slaves have mixed with other skin colors in the Americas. Mixture has resulted in the sharing and blending of physical features, so that today there are endless varieties, especially in Africa, India and Brazil. Those examples we referred to in Africa are not recent occurrences but have been there from the dawn of time.

As regards Africans and Europeans being original settlers of Africa, let us quote from *Encyclopedia Americana* (Vol. 1, 1979): "There are numerous populations, such as the Fulani in the regions just south of the Sahara in West Africa and many of the Somali, who appeared to have acquired their characteristics from both Negroid and Caucasoid ancestors and may most properly be regarded as 'mixed.' "

Even the Masai of Kenya generally have the pointed noses characteristic of Europeans. African features that appear to be "characteristic from both Negroid and Caucasoid ancestors" are not be be regarded as the result of comparatively recent mixtures of Africans and Europeans but their ancient ancestors.

The same encyclopedia states that: "The Caucasoids in sub-Sahara Africa arrived during comparatively recent times from Europe and Asia, and cannot yet be regarded as 'indigenous races.' " There are even "Bushmen" who have identical European features, such as pointed noses and tapered mouths, except for color of skin.

Thus, the original settlers were what you might call a "mixture" of Europeans, Orientals, and Africans. The same is true of Asia and Europe.

Europe

The European cannot boast of "purity of race." Several authorities could be cited to prove that Europeans, although now predominantly white, are of mixed origin, including blacks. One such authority is UNESCO in their book, *The Race Question in Modern Science:*

> The people of Europe are of such mongrel origin that any attempt at classification according to only two characteristics (color of eyes and hair) would exclude two-thirds of the population in any region studied; the addition of a third characteristic (cranial formation or skull) would leave us with a still smaller fraction of the population presenting the required combination of all the three characteristics; and with the inclusion of stature and nasal index, the proportion of pure types would become infinitesimal . . .
>
> Moreover the existence of *Negroid and Mongoloid* races in prehistoric Europe is a further proof that cross-breeding is not a recent phenomenon, and that the *oldest* populations of Europe are no more than the product of such miscegenation over thousands of years.[1] (Italics ours).

Also, the Scandinavians mixed conjugally with the Eskimos, and there is great diversity in Siberian regions, where practically all colors are represented. In view of the foregoing, Europe certainly cannot boast of purity of race, including Germany of Hitler's day and today.

India

India is considered to be made up of six distinctively different "racial strains," embracing practically all the varieties that are to be found in the human family today. Varying facial structures, colors and textures of hair and so forth are to be found in India. There are Indians who have the facial appearances of Japanese, Chinese or Koreans. Then there are those who might be called "Caucasians" or whites. All of these are indigenous settlers of India.

China And Japan

"Racially, the Chinese are a mixed people. That much we know," says K. S. Latourette in his book, *The Chinese History and Culture.*

"It would be a mistake to think that the Chinese people are all of one race," says *Catholic Encyclopedia* (Vol. 3, 1967).

Another example of thorough mixing is found among the Ainus of Japan. The Ainus are thought to be the early inhabitants of Japan. They are about 20,000 in number. Most of the Ainus live in the northernmost mainland of Japan's city of Hokkaido. As we have discussed in Chapter Four, anthropologists believe that the Ainus are related to the Europeans; others say that they are related to the Asians or the Australian Aborigines. The Ainus, like all others, are part of the one human family. Now the majority of Ainus have "intermarried," "intermixed," or "interbred" with the Japanese. Where, then, do we draw the line of demarcation? Are the Japanese a mixture of Europeans, other Asians, Australian Aborigines, or what?

During World War II, the U.S. occupied Japan. This led to the "interbreeding" of American soldiers with Japanese women. Of course, since then, there are many Americans who have married Japanese and Vietnamese women. The Americans and Canadians have also thoroughly "mixed" with American Indians and the Hawaiians.

North America

We all know that the U.S. is often referred to as "a nation of immigrants." True to that phrase, people living in the U.S. come from all over the world. All these interbreed, and white masters in the South cohabited with black women and produced offspring. At what point does one "cease being a Negro (as if inferior) or a white man (as if superior)?"

Many of those who segregate themselves on the basis of racial superiority may have been the offspring of recent "mixtures," but certainly products of mixtures from "the oldest population of Europe," which has been established to include Negroids.

Mexico And Brazil

There are infinite varieties and mixtures of people in Central and South America. In Mexico there are Japanese Mexicans, Chinese Mexicans and so forth. However, Brazil is the most "mixed" country in South America. Regarding this, *Encyclopedia Britannica* says: "At a very early stage the Portuguese mixed with the Indians, as well as with the Africans. Ethnic elements that have remained unmixed are rare today. On the contrary, all kinds of categories are represented, and the Brazilian population offers an infinity of shadings" (Vol. 15, 1987).

Jamaica

"Out of many, one people" is the theme of Jamaica's national anthem. That speaks for mixtures of blacks, Portuguese, East Indians, Chinese, Lebanese and other Europeans. The same holds true for the other islands of the Caribbean.

South Pacific

"The racial composition of the peoples of Oceania is a composite of Caucasoid, Mongoloid, and Negroid elements," says *Encyclopedia Brittanica* (Vol. 13, 1978). Anthropologists agree that the original inhabitants reached the Pacific Islands from mainland Asia.

All kinds of hair color and textures, eyes, noses, and skin colors are represented in the Pacific Islands. It is appropriate then for the same authority to say: "In general, notions of a series of massive migrations, of relatively pure racial types from the Asian continent and there miscegenation with antecedent peoples, seem to most specialists today to be simplistic."

The more than five hundred languages spoken in Melanesia, Micronesia and Polynesia are not of African or European origin, though some of the people display both African and European characteristics in their makeups; rather their languages are Asiatic, especially those of Indonesia, which seems to indicate that on their migratory journey from mainland Asia, Indonesia was one of their last settlements before they took to the water to settle on thousands of South Pacific Islands.

Australia

There were about 300,000 Aborigines in Australia when the Europeans arrived in 1788. Many Aborigines were killed, starved to death or otherwise destroyed. Now, two hundred years later, there are only about 140,000 Aborigines remaining in Australia. Many of these have "intermarried" with Europeans and adopted European customs so that today there are many apparently white Australians who, in reality, are part Aborigine and part European.

The Maoris Of New Zealand

Another example is found in New Zealand. When the Europeans set foot in New Zealand in 1769, there were about 250,000 Maoris in this land. These Polynesians, like Australian Aborigines, were decimated through violent means similar to those engaged in against the Australian Aborigines. Today, however, there are about 40,000 Maoris left in New Zealand. Just as in Australia, those left have "intermarried" with Europeans.

The Jews

Even the Jews, now dispersed among ninety countries, and long kept separated by the Mosaic law, cannot boast of "pure race" from their beginning as a people or as a nation.

The twelve sons of Jacob constitute the twelve tribes of Israel. Joseph was one of the twelve sons of Jacob. However, Joseph married an Egyptian named Asenath, the daughter of Potphera, an Egyptian priest of the ancient city of On.[2] (See Genesis 41:45, 50; 46:20). Ephraim and Manasseh, the two sons of Joseph, born to him by his Egyptian wife, together constituted one of the twelve tribes of Israel. And can we safely assume that during the four hundred years the Israelites were slaves in Egypt, they did not intermarry with Egyptians?

According to 1 Chronicles 7:14, Manasseh had a Syrian concubine. When the Israelites left Egypt, "with them too went a large company of every kind" to the Promised Land (Exo. 12:38). And the Israelites have continued to mix with others. Today, although belligerent towards each other, the Israelis, the Egyptians and the Palestinians have intermarried. Therefore, it is not uncommon for an Egyptian to have a Jewish last name and vice versa. Also, there are Jewish communities in Egypt and Egyptians and other nationalities living in Israel. All these, expectedly, intermarry and have children.

What conclusion, then, must we reach? "We may take it then," says the book *The Race Question in Modern Science,* by UNESCO, "that there are no pure races; the very most it would be possible to define a pure race is in terms of the incidence of one selected somatic characteristic, but *never* in terms of all or even of the majority of hereditary traits." [3]

Long isolation of some groups have made possible such similar physical characteristics as we shall see.

"Admixture," "intermixture," "interbreed," "miscegenation" and other "mixing" terms are really unnecessary because mankind was already an inseparable whole from the beginning. The only way a person can attempt to separate himself from the one and only human family is to commit suicide, and even then billions had already helplessly settled in the soil before him. Separating oneself otherwise is forever late—as late as bringing time back so that yesterday is not yesterday, or to be able to recall and rearrange events that have already occurred thousands of years ago to suit one's selfish cravings. What human can perform such a phenomenon?

MIGRATION

Another cause of intermixing and interbreeding is migration. Migration, especially in ancient times, usually results in crossbreeding between groups. People migrate for various reasons: curiosity, adventure, dramatic changes in climate, and natural disasters. Confusion of a common language resulted in the scattering and subsequent migrating of people from the Plains of Shinar or Babel. Migration can also be impelled by famine, war, and so forth. Examples are to be seen all over the world, and they create a fertile ground for "interbreeding."

Take, as an example, migration to the Americas from other parts of the world. In modern times there have been debates about pre-Columbian cultures and Indo-European civilizations in general, but the existence in Mexico and Central America (among the Mayas, Aztecs and the Incas) of terraced edifices, like the Sumeria ziggurats, calendrical systems, mathematics, sculptured figures with beards indicate to scholars a connection with the Assyrians, Phoenicians, Hittites, Babylonians, and the Carthaginians—all from Asia except the latter who were located in the northernmost tip of Africa. Other artifacts, such as the Meso-American art, whose features include lotus blossoms, tree-of-life designs, scrolls, and sea monsters, are viewed by many scholars as strong evidence of massive migration to the Americas from India, China, Japan and Southeast Asia. In 1872, inscriptions were found on a stone at Paraiba, Brazil, interpreted to be of

Canaanite origin.

A study of the Mayan civilization and those of other early Central American dwellers have shown that they were, undoubtedly, from Asia and were of a variety of skin colors. Regarding the origin of the Mayas, Sylvanus Griswold Morley says:

> Two other physical characteristics of the modern Maya suggest the northeastern Asiatic origin which they share with other American Indian groups: (1) the epicanthic eye fold, and (2) the Mongolian spot. The epicanthic fold is a fold at the inner corner of the eye which is characteristic of eastern Asiatics; it is also common among the modern Yucatan Maya. Judging by its frequency in representations of the face in sculptures and paintings, it must also have been a prevalent characteristic in ancient times.[4]

In North America, burial mounds in the Mississippi Valley have yielded tablets interpreted to be of Arabic, Chinese, Hebrew, Greek, Celtic, Sumerian and Gaelic origins. Monoliths (stone pillars or monuments, or masonry, or statues) found along the eastern coast of the U.S. are believed to have Viking origin. So, all early migrations to the Americas point mainly to Asia as the base from which people emanated.

FIRST SELF-DISCOVERY

You may recall that we raised provocative questions in the earlier part of this chapter under the subheading "In Search of Racial Purity Around the Globe." We propounded these questions: "Were *whites* the *only* original inhabitants of Europe? Were *blacks* the only original inhabitants of Africa?"

We have quoted *Encyclopedia Americana* as saying that the original inhabitants of Africa had "characteristics from both Negroid and Caucasoid ancestors," and that "some Cushites [or Ethiopians] are predominantly Caucasoid in race." We quoted Unesco, *The Race Question in Modern Science,* as saying, among other things, that "the *existence of Negroid* and *Mongoloid* races in pre-historic Europe is a further proof that cross-breeding is not a recent phenomenon, and that the *oldest* population of Europe are no more than the product of miscegenation [interbreeding between members of different races] over thousands of years."

The conclusion reached in the previous paragraph is food for thought, but not easily digestible. Perhaps we can nibble at it by seasoning it with some questions: If truly the original inhabitants of Europe and Africa were once both blacks and whites, at what point in history did this take place? Why is it that we do not today have an indigenous white African country, and a black European country?

To answer the first question, we simply do not know at what point in human history both blacks and whites lived in Europe as original settlers. Our UNESCO quotation mentions "pre-historic Europe" and "over thousands of years" that this comprised the "oldest" population of Europe.

While we do not know at what point blacks and whites were the original inhabitants of Europe and Africa, we can present logical evidence about *how* it may have happened.

People (originally of the same color) undoubtedly settled in areas with various climatic conditions as they migrated from an original spot in Asia to other parts of Asia and the rest of the world. Over a long period of time the migrants developed ways of life which we now call cultures. But those who migrated to warm climatic regions had also developed dark skin pigmentation, and those who migrated to moderately cold climates developed yellow pigmentation.

Yet migration did not stop—an act that is "as old as the human race." In the process of migrating back and forth, different color groups settled together. Take the Cushites as an example: "Some Cushites [blacks who once settled in Ethiopia but now are scattered among African tribes] are predominantly Caucasoid in race, but nearly all groups have undergone some degree of mixture with Negroids" (*Encyclopedia Americana*, Vol. 15, 1978).

Regarding all human populations, *Encyclopedia Britannica* comments: "*All* human populations are of mixed origin. The problem of research is to discover when and with whom" (Vol. 15, 1978).

Latourette says: "South China was quite probably once peopled, at least in part, by negritos (small blacks or pygmies) of types similar to those still found in some of the islands of Southeast Asia," [5] especially the Philippines, and the East Indies.

Because different colors migrated back and forth, "Negroid and Mongoloid races" were among the original settlers of Europe, and whites were among the original inhabitants of Africa. What is true of Europe and Africa is also true of other parts of the world. We might call this admixture the first self-discovery.

SELF-REDISCOVERY

It appears, however, that there was a long period during which virtually no long distance migration occurred. Groups established their own boundaries, and the boundaries eventually resulted in the nations or countries we have today. But as man's needs grew and could not be completely met by farming and hunting, the necessity to travel arose. So people traveled, either to sell their goods or to seek raw materials for rapidly developing industries.

Britain is a classic example of a country which needed to venture beyond its shores in order to survive. And venture it did, which is why Britain used to "rule the waves." The need for survival brought the British in close contact with other nations—nations which eventually became part of the British Empire upon which "the sun never set."

As the Europeans voyaged, they discovered concentrations of people who were either black or yellow. They spoke different languages and could not relate to each other culturally. Hence, the question of race and communality of origin of man became a subject of controversy.

Since this second rediscovery, the relationship among colors of skin has not been the same. But these people of different colors were among the "oldest" ancestors of the Europeans. On the other hand, the Europeans were among the indigenous inhabitants of Africa. In any event, that was a second discovery—when whites came into contact face to face with concentrations of yellow and black people.

Now to our second question: Why is it that we do not have today an indigenous white African country or black European country[6] if truly the oldest ancestors of Europe were people of different colors, including black? Simply because whites who migrated to Africa in pre-historic times would have turned black long before the second self-rediscovery. The part which climate plays in skin pigmentation has been amply discussed in Chapter Three.

But what about "the existence of Negroid and Mongoloid races in pre-historic Europe?" Should there not be a part of Europe still occupied by blacks or orientals since these were among the oldest populations of Europe?

"Pre-historic Europe" existed how many thousands of years ago? Since it was a pre-historic period, it does not seem anybody knows for certain. In the days of Jesus Christ, about two thousand years ago, Europe was a thriving society, for Rome was a world power, and Britain was part of its colonies. Greece was a world power before Rome, and Greece's secular history extends eight centuries B.C.E. So pre-historic Europe could be a period as long as four or five thousand years ago.

During such possible long stretch of time, several things could have happened to the inhabitants of pre-historic Europe: fierce warring tribes could have subjugated or eliminated other tribes; the "Negroid and Mongoloid races" could have migrated to other parts of the world, especially to Asia and Africa; and, very importantly, they would have interbred with or assimilated by dominant color groups living in Europe then, for, as noted on page 89, "the people of Europe are of such mongrel origin [or mixed breed] that any classification according to only two characteristics (color of eyes and hair) would exclude two-thirds of the population in any region studied" as of pure race. If a third characteristic, "cranial formation," and a fourth characteristic, "nasal index" were to be included, "the proportion of pure types [of people in Europe] would become infinitesimal." [7]

During the thousands of years of interbreeding in pre-historic Europe (or in Africa and Asia) blending of skin colors and physical characteristics would no doubt had taken place. The surviving dominant color group would naturally be determined by the interaction of the then prevailing climatic influence on skin color. For these reasons, we do not have today, a black European country or an indigenous white African country. (See Chapter Three for the discussion of how climate would have affected the ancient inhabitants of the tropics and temperate regions of the world.)

So whether people are called Orientals or Asians, Europeans or Russians, Africans, North or Latin Americans, Caribbeans or are identified with the thousands of islands of the South Pacific and the Atlantic, they belong to the one and only one human race that is now thoroughly mixed, and will continue to be so.

Appropriately, Professors Asimov and Boyd noted: "For that reason there are always questions as to whether an individual or even a group of individuals belong to one race or another." [8]

We will also go along with Professor Bentley Glass who said: "The chasm between human races and peoples, where it exists, is psychological and sociological, it is not genetics!" [9] Therefore, to say that one is superior to others is a feeling and not fact.

Suppose you have, all your life, believed in the superiority of one people or color over another? What should you do now? Should you continue tenaciously to cling to your view? Let us listen to the advice of Boyd and Asimov:

> From all we know about genetics today, then, we can say that anyone who believes in "race superiority" is igno-

rant or misled. There is still no scientific evidence for superiority or inferiority of any race.

You may be telling yourself at this point: There doesn't
seem to be much to this notion of race if it tells us so little.

And that is exactly what we must realize. The whole
notion of race is really quite useless to the average man.
Except for certain unscientific and superstitious ideas, it
tells him nothing. The notion of race is useful only to
anthropologists and so forth. The rest of us might as well
stop worrying about the whole thing.

We should consider human beings as individuals to be
judged for themselves alone, and not as members of any
race. This is not only the kindest way to behave, but also,
as this book tried to show, the most scientific way as
well.[10]

But why, in the first place, is there confusion about the
human race?

WHY THE CONFUSION

For various reasons uncertainty exists among many people
about mankind being from the same parents and all being equal
in every way. First of all, great intervals of time had passed since
the dispersion of mankind from Babel. During this long interval of
separation, many changes had taken place, including changes in
skin pigmentation, hair color and texture, and the shape and size
of facial characteristics. Languages, too, have multiplied several
times; different customs or cultures and ways of worship have
developed; values and philosophical outlooks on life and living
have all taken different and radical turns. The great distances
which separated people from one another also played a significant
role. For one thing, great distances which exist, especially between
peoples of different color groups, language groups and so forth,
produce a sense of not belonging, or as if color-groups developed
separately and independently of each other.

GENERAL CONCLUSION

In view of what we have considered, what conclusion have you
reached about the existence of a "pure" or "master" race?

The *World Book Encyclopedia* (Vol. 16, 1984) points out:
"People often speak of the 'German race,' the 'Italian race,' or the
'Welsh race.' There are no such races, though there may be more
or less subpopulations in those countries. [For example] there is

no single Jewish race . . . Neither is there a single black race."

"There is no evidence," declares *Encyclopedia Americana* (Vol. 23, 1979), "that . . . any pure race ever existed except in the imagination of race classifiers; the facts available are rather against this view. The racial variation is a dynamic expression of the changing pattern of gene frequencies in the human species."

Dr. Montagu says, "In the first UNESCO statement on race, paragraph six reads as follows: 'National, religious, geographic, linguistic and cultural groups do not necessarily coincide with racial groups; and cultural traits of such groups have no demonstrated genetic connection with racial traits. Because serious errors of this kind are habitually committed when the term "race" is used in popular parlance, it would be better when speaking of human races to drop the term "race" altogether and speak of ethnic groups.' " [11]

What, then, are we going to do with the word "race"?

OUST IT!

We do not want to be biased about the word race. We must, therefore, listen to the opinions and conclusions of respected scientists and doctors:

Kalmus writes: "It is customary to discuss the local variety of humanity in terms of "race." However, it is unnecessary to use this *greatly debased word,* [12] since it is easy to describe population without it." [13]

Professor Ernst Handart said that he did not believe that there are any "true races" in mankind.[14]

Professor L.S. Penrose concluded that he did not "see the necessity for the rather apologetic retention of the obsolete term race." [15] "Obsolete" because the available scientific knowledge unmistakably shows that there is but one human race regardless of superficial physical differences.

Dr. J.P. Garlick observed that "the use of race as a taxonomic ["systematic scientific classification or grouping or naming, especially of biological creatures"] unit for man seems *out-of-date, if not irrational."* [16]

Professor P.A. Parsons encouraged: "There are good arguments for abandoning the term race, as it is clearly *arbitrary, undefinable, and without biological meaning."* [17]

"Undefinable"? Why? Simply because there is no line of demarcation by which people could be properly classified as belonging to this "race" or that "race," as we have already considered. What is more, the ancestors of those who claim white or other colors today may have been intermixed with blacks, Orientals, American Indians and Spanish.

It is "without biological meaning" because all people, everywhere, are basically anatomically the same. In other words, all color-groups possess the same physical and mental characteristics.

Therefore, such terms as black race, white race, Orientals, Hispanic or Chicano, Caucasians or Caucasoids, Negroes or Negroids, Negritos, Mongols or Mongoloids, Multiracial and so forth are misnomers. Even the words black race and white race are misnomers. Not all who are referred to as blacks are really black. There are brown, copper-brown, yellow, blue-black and so forth. Not all whites are of the same shade; some are darker than others just as their hair color is not the same. There are no groups of people living on the planet earth that have identical color. Even the intensity of color of skin and hair can differ among children whose parents have the same color of skin and hair, and are born in the same environment.

We will now examine the deplorable conditions which exist in South Africa. Can such conditions be attributed to a curse or mental inferiority?

NOTES

1. UNESCO, *The Race Question in Modern Science*, (New York, Whitside & Morrow, 1956), p. 18.

2. On is now destroyed, and to be found on its location is a village called Matariyah.

3. UNESCO, p. 18.

4. Sylvanus Griswold Morley, *The Ancient Maya*, (Stanford, Stanford University Press, 1956), p. 24.

5. Kenneth Scott Latourette, *The Chinese, Their History and Culture*, Vol. 2, (New York, Macmillan, 1934), p. 2.

6. As we all know, the Europeans living in Africa and other hot climatic regions of the world settled in those areas in relatively modern times.

7. UNESCO, p. 18.

8. *Races and People*, p. 55.

9. Bentley Glass, "Genes and the Man," (New York, Columbia University Press, 1943), pp. 173-74.

10. *Races and People*, p. 167-68.

11. *Man's Most Dangerous Myth*, p. 435.

12. All italics in the following series of quotations are ours.

13. H. Kalmus, *Variation and Heredity*, (London, Routledge and K. Paul, 1958), p. 30.

14. Ernst Handart, *Infectious Diseases*, in A. Sorsby ed. Clinical Genetics (London, Butterworths Pub., 1973), p. 545.

15. L.S. Penrose in "Annals of Eugenics," Vol. 17, Part 3, Feb. 1953, (London, Cambridge University Press), p. 253.

16. J.P. Garlick "Annals of Human Genetics," Vol. 25, Part 2, Oct. 1961, (London, Cambridge University Press), p. 169.

17. P.A. Parsons, "Genetics Determination of Behavior (Mice and Men)," in Ehrman, Omenn, and Caspari eds, Genetics, Environment, and Behavior, (New York, Academic Press, 1972), p. 94.

EIGHT

WHAT ABOUT THE OPPRESSION OF BLACKS IN SOUTH AFRICA?

'All laws are for whites and all orders are for blacks,' commented Bill Moyers of CBS on the apartheid regime. The orders are ruthless. That is the situation in South Africa. And, as you are well aware, both the laws and the orders are issued by white South Africans. Yet the white population in South Africa is currently only about 6 million, whereas the black population is 22 million. The Coloreds' (those of mixed race with whites, blacks and Indians) population is about 3-1/2 million, and Asians number one million.[1] In spite of their relatively small population, the whites have ruled black South Africans for centuries.

Out of the 472,359 square miles (1,221,042 sq km) land area that constitutes South Africa, whites claim 80 percent of the land and blacks are confined to about fourteen percent of the land. Yet blacks constitute about eighty percent of the population of South Africa. Suppose 22 million Americans ruled the U.S. and confined the other 193 million (1984 figure) to either New England or California.

But the 25 million non-white South Africans are confined mostly to unproductive areas of land, such as the mountainous, sparsely vegetated and hard-packed soils. As would be expected, the choicest portions of the land are grabbed by whites. Also, blacks are often forced out of parts of their bleak land if precious minerals are discovered there or if blacks make the land attractive and productive. The ruling minority cannot tolerate such an advancement by blacks. Nonetheless, blacks have not, in spite of their relentless struggle, been able to effect significant changes in the South African government's iron-fisted ruling policies.

Since it has been firmly established that all peoples are equal physically and mentally, it is no great surprise that many, including blacks themselves, have wondered if blacks were truly cursed to be servants to the whites. Before we consider why blacks find it very difficult to free themselves from the tyranny of white minority rule, let us see some of what blacks go through under the South African regime.

APARTHEID, A REIGN OF TERROR?

Apartheid is a system of rule that is operative only in South Africa. Apartheid is an Afrikaans word which means "apart-ness." Some people, especially in South Africa, preferring euphemism, would like to define apartheid as "separate development," or separate economic, educational, and cultural development for the different ethnic groups in South Africa.

However, *Encyclopedia Americana* (Vol. 2, 1979) shows how grossly misleading "separate development" is when talking about apartheid:

> Apartheid involves more than separation. The white population of South Africa occupies a position of supremacy, based on history and custom and buttressed by law. The central government has the sovereign powers over the entire country, including the Transkei.[2] Only whites may be members of Parliament and the cabinet. Members of Parliament are elected by white voters or appointed by the government—except four, who are elected by colored voters. African chiefs are paid by the government and may be dismissed by the government. The major organizations opposed to apartheid are banned; many individual opponents of the doctrine are imprisoned or otherwise silenced. African trade unions are not recognized in industrial bargaining. Only whites may possess firearms or be arms-carrying members of the military and police forces.

Echoing opinion similar to the one expressed above is the *New Republic*: "Whites in South Africa are not only a small minority—four million people, as opposed to 20 million nonwhites; they also control virtually all wealth and, absolutely, all political power."[3]

It is obvious from the above quotes that political, military, judicial and economical powers are employed by the government of South Africa to crush opposers of apartheid. Actions that have been taken in South Africa to silence opponents of the apartheid regime include restrictions, imprisonment, or confinement to one's home.

Prominent among opponents of apartheid is Nelson Mandela, who had spent twenty-seven years in prison before he was released in February of 1990. His wife, Winnie Mandela, has been, until relatively recently, banished to her house since 1977; she has spent seventeen months in solitary confinement jail. All of these restrictive measures and many more are employed by the South African government to repress people.

Others have been silenced by death. Such was the fate of Steven Biko, called "an apostle of nonviolence." Ironically, he died a violent death in the hands of the authorities. About his death, *Newsweek* reported:

> Early that morning [of Biko's funeral], the Johannesburg Sunday Express had reported for the first time allegations that Biko had not died from a prison hunger strike as police had asserted, but of massive brain damage. As the mourners filed past the coffin, they could see a huge bump on his left temple; the back of Biko's skull was so badly crushed that it had to be concealed with velvet.[4]

A white South African who attempted to uncover the mystery behind the death of Biko is living in political asylum in the United States.

However, recent reports have removed the official veil shrouding the cause of Biko's death, which was originally attributed to heart and kidney failure. The cause of death has now been attributed to brutal beatings, especially to the head. *The New York Times* of October 17, 1985, reported that the doctor (Tucker) who examined Biko gave a false medical report about the cause of his death. The *Times* reported Biko as "frothing [foaming] at the mouth and hyperventilating and had collapsed." In this physical state Biko was "taken 800 miles, naked and manacled in the back of a Land-Rover, from Port Elizabeth to Pretoria and died the next day."[5]

On October 21, 1985, Benjamin Mloisi was hanged for murdering a policeman. Mr. Mloisi denied the murder charge, and South African authorities denied Mrs. Mloisi the opportunity of seeing her son before or after he was hanged. She was told that the corpse was "state property" and that she could return in about a week "to pick up a grave number" of her son. At least eighty-six blacks have been executed in 1987.

To Maintain Law And Order Or To Kill—Which?

In 1976 Africans in the Johannesburg Soweto township rioted to show their discontent at classes in African schools being taught in Afrikaans.[6] About six hundred demonstrators were killed by police during the riot. Only a handful were white. For example, out of 176 killed in one area of Soweto, only two of them were white.

It was clear, especially in view of the large number killed, that the main interest of the police was not to contain the crowd but to kill. Confirming this was a white eyewitness of the Soweto riot. She said, "It was obvious that the police weren't there to practice crowd control but to kill." After identifying the body of her eighteen-year-old daughter, a woman sobbed, "Her body has many bullet holes." [7]

Proving further that the police were more interested in killing than in restoring law and order was shown by the African riot in the same township of Soweto in 1960. Police fired indiscriminately into the rioting crowd. Result: sixty-nine blacks were killed; one hundred and eighty-six injured.

In recent waves of racial riots in South Africa, about 2,000 persons have been killed over a two-year period, up to June, 1986. Only one of those was white—a soldier. In conditions that are normal by South African standards, blacks are killed every day on racial ground. By 1985 the racial unrest had taken a dramatic turn for the worse; several blacks were gunned down every day by police. On only one night in August, 1985, nine blacks were reported killed by the South Africa military and police. The main social events among black South Africans have become funeral processions. Among those gunned down were boys ten and four years old. On another occasion, an eighteen-month-old baby was shot and killed either by a soldier or a police officer. If the shooting was not an accident (and it was not reported to be), how great a threat was an infant less than two years old to South African police or military muscle? Nonetheless, the indiscriminate killings continue. Or as a South African put it: "They regard brutality as law and order."

Ruthless Destruction Of Women And Children

An International Seminar on Women, Children and Apartheid in South Africa made this observation, as reported by the *U.N. Chronicle* of July, 1980: "The seminar drew particular attention to the crimes of the apartheid regime in killing and maiming women

August 13, 1976, Capetown, South Africa: Police beat a student protestor at the University of Western Cape. Seventeen arrests were made during anti-government riots. (Bettmann Archives)

August 25, 1976, Johannesburg, South Africa: Residents drag away a dead man in coveralls in the black township of Soweto after police fired into a crowd of demonstrators. (Bettmann Archives)

the crimes of the apartheid regime in killing and maiming women and children in peaceful demonstrations against injustice, to the forcing of thousands of villagers into concentration camps in Northern Namibia, and to the bombing of women and children in refuge centers." [8]

Various reports confirmed this crime against women and children in South Africa. For example, *Newsweek* of June 9, 1980, reported: "Bernard Fortuin, a fifteen-year-old of mixed race, was on his way to buy groceries for his mother in Elsies River, a suburb of Cape Town, when he saw other colored teenagers throwing stones at white motorists. Suddenly, one of the cars stopped. Four white policemen jumped out and opened fire with shotguns. Two youths died on the spot, including Bernard Fortuin. When his mother heard the news, she ran to the scene and, hysterical, tried to approach the body of her son. A policeman in camouflaged riot fatigues beat her back with a truncheon, shouting in Afrikaans: 'Laat die donder vrek.' ('Let the bastard die.') [9]

A fifteen-year-old boy, Freddie Williams, was reportedly shot to death by police. It was alleged that he had tried to run away after he was arrested for stealing grapes! One western diplomat said, "This is tense as hell—you can feel it." The condition at this time of writing is more than tense; it is mind-numbing.

Reported *New Republic* of July 19, 1980: "A white police constable, H.du Toit, has told a court he did not intervene when he saw a white man beating a black man because he 'didn't want to get involved.' He allowed, however, that he felt 'a bit guilty' about his inaction because he was in a government car at the time. The black man, Mojakwena James Oliphant, died two days later from his injuries." [10]

We are left to wonder: If the black man had been beating up the white man, would the police officer have gotten "involved" or indifferently overlooked the melee?

The 184-page report entitled "The War Against Children: South Africa's Youngest Victims" describes some of the barbarous and sickening crimes committed against black children by South African's police and soldiers. Here are excerpts of the report, printed in the *New York Times* of April 18, 1986 and the *Los Angeles Times* of the same date and month:

> South Africa's black children are routinely being beaten, shot, whipped and arrested by the country's security forces, according to a report issued today by a group of American lawyers.
> The South African police, in a statement issued in Pretoria, rejected the report's findings.

The report compiled by the New York-based Lawyers Committee for Human Rights said, "More than 200 children have been killed in the past year and hundreds more have been injured in police operations in the townships in which tear gas, birdshot, rubber bullets, sjamboks and even live ammunition are used indiscriminately and excessively." Sjamboks are metal-tipped whips.

"In large-scale and often arbitrary police action, thousands of children, some as young as seven years old, have been arrested and detained pursuant to South Africa's sweeping security and criminal legislation. Hundreds of students, including many who did not participate in school boycotts, have been arrested; others have been killed or wounded."

"In an introduction to the lawyers' report, Bishop Desmond Tutu, the anti-apartheid activist and Nobel Peace Prize winner, wrote of the case of a fifteen-year-old boy named Johnny who the report said was beaten by the police.

"I have seen the Johnny referred to in this book," Bishop Tutu wrote. "He spoke with great difficulty as if his tongue was swollen and filled his mouth. He had a kind of lisp as well. His eyes were dull as of someone who seemed to be dead to the world. When he walked, it was with a slow painful shuffle like a punchdrunk ex-boxer."

The 184-page report details dozens of individual cases in which it said children were killed by security forces or arrested and tortured. "A generation of children is growing up in South Africa knowing nothing but the daily violence of the white minority regime," the report said.

"At times," the report said, "violence against children has been the result of a deliberate strategy of the security forces to suppress student organizations and protests. In their frequent sweeps and patrols through the townships, security forces have singled out young people of school age for arrest, pursuing them with sjamboks—metal-tipped whips—and shooting at random at any child who runs away."

In reporting on individual cases, the report said children and parents were reluctant to permit their names to be used for fear of retribution by security forces. In the case of a boy named Martin who was arrested with a friend and accused of stoning a vehicle, the report quotes Martin's account of his arrest:

"They started sjambokking me all over the body. I fell down, and they started kicking me all over while I was lying down. I stood up, and he sjambokked me on the left ear. I was bleeding profusely by then. We were never taken to a doctor."

In another case, the report quotes from the statement of a girl named Miriam, 12, who was shot on June 17, 1985, as she was going home from a bread shop:

"I saw a white policeman come out of a house I was running past. He had a long gun. I was alone in the street and ran faster, still holding the bread. I did not hear any call from the policeman. As I reached the corner of Fifth Avenue, I heard one bang and felt a terrible pain in my lower back. I fell. I was in terrible pain, but conscious. I felt where the pain was in my back and saw that my hand was bloody."

The report said children who have been detained are often mistreated. "Children who have been arrested are routinely subjected to physical assault by the security forces at the time of arrest and in the early stages of custody," it said." [11]

The *Los Angeles Times* reported cases "of children who were beaten, whipped, abused sexually, deprived for days of sleep and food and tortured with electric shocks."

One of such children was Joseph, fourteen. While playing soccer he was yanked away by soldiers. The soldiers inflicted on him a series of abuses.

"A white soldier took my right arm and bent it behind my back," Joseph said. The soldier reached into his pocket and pulled out a cigarette lighter. Joseph said he could smell his flesh as the soldier held the lighter beneath his right wrist. Then a wire was tied around his right hand, water was poured on his body and the boy was repeatedly treated with electric shocks. As his body shook, Joseph's thumbnail ripped off and the nail took a chunk of flesh along with it. Then the soldiers lacerated his body with broken bottles.

Joseph's hands were wrenched out of shape and his body blackened by the repeated electric shocks, and his body was disfigured by the cuts and burns.

Another boy, Eugene Vusi Diamini, was arrested by six policemen. First, he was beaten, then his mouth was stuffed with the inner tube of a tire. Thereupon the officers began to kick and punch him in the stomach. He was battered until he lost consciousness.

When he regained conciousness the police officers blindfolded him, strapped him to a chair, hand and foot, drenched him with water and then repeatedly shocked him with electric current.

Ditwe was fifteen. After his arrest, he bled from being beaten, whipped and kicked. His arms were broken and plastic whips left deep gashes on his chest and back. He was allowed to see a doctor—five days later!

As for Zukizani, sixteen, the police played a game of cruelty with him: Zukizani was held hands and feet, spread apart on all fours, tossed into the air and let go. As he lay on the floor where he crashed, police officers would stand on his back or stomach—depending on which side he landed.

In 1985 twelve persons died while detained without trial under South Africa security law. Three of these were reported to be minors. Who or what killed them? Law enforcement officers were not obligated by law to account for the death of detainees! [12]

According to the U.N. publication, *Apartheid in Practice*, hundreds of laws are enforced with the single-minded view of repressing, destroying physically, mentally and morally South African blacks. Here are a few of the laws:

- No African black male, even if he is legally residing in a town by virtue of a permit, is allowed to have his wife and children reside with him without a permit.
- Police are empowered, without a warrant, to search at any reasonable time of day or night, the premises of an African youth aged 18 and under if the police have reason to suspect that the youth is committing a criminal offense by living with his (or her) father without a permit to do so.
- A person who breaks a window of a private or public building in the course of a demonstration demanding more rights for blacks, if found guilty, has committed "sabotage." It is punishable by death.
- A white person is guilty of a criminal offense if he or she attempts to teach a black African how to read or write.
- A black African who attends, without permission, even a single lecture at a university designated for whites is guilty of a criminal offense punishable by a heavy fine.
- According to The Terrorism Act of 1967, if a person has written letters to Africans, which letters are deemed to arouse hostility between whites and other color-groups in South Africa, the person has committed a criminal act that is punishable by death.

- Under the same Terrorism Act a person may be detained indefinitely in solitary confinement without trial. Persons detained may mysteriously disappear. Police are not required by law to account for the fate of a detainee. (The Terrorism Act, though enacted in 1967, was made to apply retroactively to offenses committed from June of 1962.)

"These [laws] and many more equally as devastating, are enforced regularly, usually rigidly, often ruthlessly." [13]

FOURTEEN NATIONS IN THE BOSOM OF ONE COUNTRY!

To further helplessly incapacitate South African blacks and non-whites, other drastic measures are employed by the South African government. The South African blacks are regarded not as one people, but as ten nations!

Regarding this view of South African government, *The World Book Encyclopedia* (Vol. 18, 1980) says: "The government regards black populations as ten separate nations, each with its own ancestry and culture."

Hence the South African government has assigned scattered reserves to the Africans, the Indians, and the Coloreds, which they refer to as "nations." One color group is prohibited from living in the section of other color groups without a permit.

They say there is strength in unity. On the other hand, if people are arbitrarily scattered into forced settlements, you weaken them. To hopelessly weaken non-whites is exactly the objective of South African government. That is why non-whites are settled into separate lands and are not permitted by law to intersettle. Even if they want to intersettle, where is the room to do so? As if confining eighty percent of the non-white population of South Africa into only thirteen percent of the land is not evil enough, the blacks are also split into two hundred sixty-five scattered settlements.

Bophuthatswana is a case in point. The South African government—though no other governments—regards Bophuthatswana as an "independent nation." Independent! Before you exclaim hurrah, listen to this: The South African government has subdivided the "independent nation" into seven scattered reserves, and the reserves are under the unfriendly scrutiny of the government. An additional two hundred black settlements are under the threat of removal. The mobility of those living in the scattered reserves, whether the reserves are independent or not, are severely restricted by the "Pass Law."

The "Pass Law" [14]

The "Pass Law" is one out of the multitude of laws used by the South African government to throw blacks into jail by the thousands each year. The law requires non-white South Africans to carry an identity card wherever they go, and also greatly restricts non-whites from venturing into white residential areas. For non-whites to go to white areas without a permit is a criminal offense. However, whites can go anywhere they want with impunity. Except for police and soldiers who make their frequent visits sharply felt, there is only one other thing to see in black settlements: human misery.

Be that as it may, how rigidly was the Pass Law enforced? In 1979, 272,887 blacks were arrested under the shackle of the law, and about half were sentenced to jail. In 1984, 163,000 blacks were arrested for looking for jobs in areas reserved for whites. It has been estimated that, on the average, three blacks were arrested every minute. Through 1985, over eighteen million blacks had been arrested, which implies that every adult black in South Africa may have been arrested at one time or another.

When arrested, people are often detained indefinitely without trial, and without opportunity to see a lawyer or members of their own family. For example, in the first ten months of 1984, 1,006 people were reported arrested on grounds other than looking for a job. Many of those arrested were detained without charge or trial under a sweeping security law. These included nine labor union leaders. One hundred seventy-six of the 1,006 arrested were detained, one hundred thirty-six of them in solitary confinement under the security law that permits indefinite solitary confinement without trial or charge. An additional sixteen leaders of anti-apartheid regime are on trial for treason and terrorism. If they are convicted, what would their punishment be? A heavy fine? A long-term jail or even life imprisonment? None of the above. They will be executed. We can understand, then, why Trevor Manuel of the *Los Angeles Times* called the sweeping emergency law "blatant intimidation."

The *San Diego Union* of July 2, 1986, said that an "estimated 4,000 people [are] being held under the latest emergency regulations without charges being filed." The people being held include nine hundred labor union leaders. Recently there has been one emergency law after another in South Africa.

STRIP BLACKS OF SOUTH AFRICAN CITIZENSHIP

The purpose of the "Pass Law" is more than to indiscriminately haul blacks into jail.

"The South African Government plan is," reported *Today's Education*, "for them [blacks] to evolve into Black States and to provide blacks with the rights of citizenship [in their reserves]. Consequently, when blacks are in South Africa—that is, in the urbanized commercial and industrial areas of the country—they will be aliens." [15] Which means that they will be divested of South African citizenship. Yet the blacks are tightly controlled in the impoverished lands of the so-called Independent Black States.

To achieve this diabolic objective of Independent Black States, Africans are indiscriminately dumped into the undesirable terrains reserved for them. *Time* of August 31, 1981 reported: "Last week, more than a hundred police swooped down on a black squatters' encampment near Cape Town and trucked thirteen hundred homeless black men, women and children to jail, before sending them to rural reservations." [16] Old women and children are, in particular, regarded by the government as surplus people. Able-bodied men dumped into the arid reservations stand the risk of arrest if they venture out of the reservation to the urban areas to look for a job.

RESULTS OF THE DUMPS

What has been the result of all this inhumane action?

Says the *New Republic* of July 19, 1980: "A glance at the annual survey put on by the doughty liberals at the Institute of Race Relations, is more than enough to bring painful enlightenment . . . [For example,] the forced resettlement program, which has already dumped two million [17] people into the impoverished Bantustans, continues unabated. This policy of deliberate dislocation and poverty has contributed to an astronomical crime rate: in 1976-77, there were two and one-half times as many murders here [in South Africa] as in the United States, which has eight times the population. In 1978 some 132 people, all but one of them black, were hanged." [18] (By the way, the murder rate in the U.S. in 1977 was one at about every twenty-nine minutes, day and night.)

Obviously, "apartheid seems designed specifically to inject cruel and humiliating complications into the lives of blacks." [19]

Indiscriminate jail sentences certainly complicate lives. How does South Africa rate in prison population compared with the rest of the world?

SOUTHERN AFRICAN PRISON

In proportion to its population, South Africa has the highest prison population in the world. In view of what we have been discussing, the reason for that is not too difficult to see. It is also not difficult to imagine that black South African prisoners are most likely living a life of constant torture and humiliation. If they were tortured and indiscriminately gunned down when they were *not* prisoners, can we reasonably expect better treatment for them in jail? It has, in fact, been said that blacks in South African prison yards are mistreated in ways too shameful to mention. For example, it was reported that a black South African prisoner laboring in the searing heat asked the white prison guard for a drink. The guard urinated and offered it to the black prisoner to drink. A person debased enough to treat a fellow human that way will most likely do other things just as bad or worse.

The book *Robben Island,* by Indres Naidoo, relates horrifying stories of what black South African prisoners go through. Here is one example:

When the bell rang for sleeping time at 8 p.m. with the midsummer sun still in the sky, the lights never being switched off, exhausted after the journey [to the prison yard] and all the tension, we soon fell asleep.

A loud bell at five a.m., startled us, and we staggered out of bed in a general rush to the bathroom. By the time I got to the buckets, both of them were overflowing with shit and piss, right onto the floor. It was a chaotic scene, chaps running to the taps, others not knowing where to relieve themselves, and no toilet paper around—absolutely no toilet paper. I decided to hold out.

At 5:30 our cells were opened and in walked some wardens, who chose two prisoners to carry out the buckets—the contents spilling all over the floor—and then chased us with batons out of the cells.

In the yard we found ourselves in the center of a semi-circle of wardens, and each of us had to run to a warden, who frisked us with his hands while we stretched our arms in the air, swearing at us, calling us pigs, and saying that we would die on the Island. While their hands searched our bodies in the most humiliating way possible, they told us that here the white man was boss, and they hurled as many insults at us as they could, crude insults, repeated over and over again, as though they could not be

in our presence or touch our bodies without saying something vile, reminding them and us of their power to do with
us exactly what they liked.[20]

The book tells of several occasions of prisoners being stripped
naked and subjected to gory beatings. Male prisoners are also
said to be sexually abused at will by male wardens. The 278-page
book is full of horrendous stories of life in South African jails. So
what is said here is less than a drop in a bucket of almost
unimaginable inhumane treatment.

As you can see from what we have discussed so far, a black
South African has several odds against him. These problems
include: (a) If he stays in his desert-like homeland he would not
have a job. (b) Because of so many poor people being lumped into
a relatively small space, the black South African can easily be
murdered in his house or neighborhood. (c) If he ventures out to
where he can get a job, he has an excellent chance of spending
the night, or several nights, in jail, and if convicted, more time in
jail. He may be detained in solitary confinement indefinitely. The
"Pass Law" is at work, even though supposedly repealed.

But what does a black South African go through before he is
shipped into a reservation? And if he is not housed in prison,
what kind of living conditions do the settlements offer?

HOUSING

Those hauled in trucks to their "nations" undergo terror.
Those who have not been hauled to their "nations" undergo terror
before or during the process of shipping them to reservations. Let
us take the case of a family as a typical example, as reported in
Progressive: [21]

Livionia Mandela was recovering from tuberculosis in a sani-
tarium. (The TB may have been caused in the first place by malnutrition.) Without notice, her mediocre home was leveled by a
bulldozer and she and her five children had to live in the bush for
three years, "sheltered only by a sheet of plastic." Eventually,
however, she built a shanty in a squalid community of
Modderdan, near Cape Town. The sub-standard house was razed
to the ground three years later—again without warning! Rather,
police attacked the residents with tear gas and dogs in the middle
of the night as bulldozers crushed their homes. She and her five
children fled to a church building at 4:00 a.m. She was homeless
again and fled into the bush a second time. An inspector "ripped
apart" the plastic tarp under which she and her five children were
living.

The family built another shanty in a squatter community called Unibel. Six months later, that community was invaded by police dogs and tear gas as bulldozers razed their beggarly homes. At this time the woman had a one-month-old baby. Since there was no safe place to stay, the woman and her children lived in hiding with a white family for six months. After that, her fate is anybody's guess.

Such heartless stories and even worse can be reported millions of times. For such harrowing experiences have been the fate of four million black South Africans who were forcefully transported from their country to their "nations," and this may be the fate of still many more.

In the home lands, many have no running water or inside plumbing, no electricity, no sanitary toilets or bathrooms. The people wallow in an environment ripe with disease. But what of job opportunities and wages for black South Africans?

JOB OPPORTUNITIES AMONG BLACK AND COLORED SOUTH AFRICANS

South Africa is the only country in the world that has laws against colors of skin. These laws restrict more than movements, they also severely restrict job opportunities and wages for blacks.

Millions of blacks have been condemned to their so-called homelands, but only a relative few can eke out a living from these poor reservations. For one thing, there is not enough land to offer subsistence farming to the people crammed onto a relatively small piece of land. So the majority of blacks have to leave their "nations" and go to other parts of the country to make a living. Therefore, as many as 70 percent of the black work force have to migrate back and forth from their "nations" to other parts of the country, where they often work as laborers on farms owned by whites or as servants to both wealthy and poor white households. Practically all white households in South Africa have maids. Yes, even unemployed whites or those on welfare have black servants. Many maids labor from 6:30 in the morning to 7:30 in the evening. They are allowed short breaks to eat and given only one day off a month.

What about wages? They are stripped to bare bone. A maid was reported to have been paid 20 Rands (less than $15) a month for a "standard work week of 60 hours." Yet, a few years ago it was estimated that 120 Rands (about $100) was needed to provide the meager necessities of life in South Africa. Little wonder why one nurse said: "They might as well be slaves. What they get paid isn't worth a tip." [22]

What about wages for other occupations? A black working in the city was reported to earn only 140 Rands (about $110). In 1984 the average annual income for white South African was $7,200; the average annual income for black South Africans in the same year was a mere $1,800. Nonetheless, many black wage earners support large families in their "homelands," such as Transkei or Venda, where about half of the families live on less than eight Rands (about six dollars) a month. Little wonder, then, why malnutrition abounds in the "homelands."

According to the World Health Organization, half of the children in the "homelands" will die before the age of five due to diseases caused by malnutrition. The infant mortality rate for 1979 for every 1,000 live births was as follows: whites, nineteen; Asians, thirty-seven; blacks, ninety-four. Has there been any significant change in infant mortality since? Yes, for some. Statistics in 1982 make a clear point: whites, 14.9; Asians, 25.3; blacks, 94. Indeed, twenty black South Africans die *every day* of tuberculosis.

What of the availability of doctors to various color groups? There is one doctor for every 750 white South Africans, and for non-whites, one doctor for every 25,000.

Because malnutrition can cause a malfunction in physical development and irreparable mental retardation, especially during the crucial developing years of a child, the future generation, like the present one, will be backward. Hence the chances of the oppressors having an upper hand against the oppressed are good. What is more, the tyrant can always justify his action by saying that those he rules are not mentally capable of taking care of themselves, so he regards any challenges of the way he rules as a rebellion against duly constituted authority. And such rebellion must be crushed.

Poverty shortens life span, and South Africa is no exception: "A few years ago in South Africa, the expectation of life for a black man was forty years, but it was sixty at the same time for a white man. At that time a white woman could expect twenty-five more years of life than a black woman." [23]

Even though these are 1964 statistics, the conditions of black South Africans have not improved much since. Current statistics about life span of whites and black South Africans still show a wide discrepancy.

The life span for a white South African (male and female average combined) is 70 years., but for black South Africans, it is 59 years. Thus the gap has not closed by much.

ECONOMIC ACTION AND REACTION

White South Africans are paid four times as much as non-whites. When non-whites take economic action, such as striking, in order to bridge the great economic chasm which separates them from whites, what usually happens?

Newsweek of June 9, 1980, reported: "In Durban 6,000 black textile workers struck for higher wages—and were immediately fired. In Cape Town, 800 slaughterhouse workers walked off the job in an attempt to secure higher wages and better conditions; the Colored community of the area mounted a boycott of red meat in support. At first Botha [the prime minister] vowed to investigate strikers' 'legitimate grievances.' Then he cracked down. Security police arrested 1,200 community leaders, teachers, students in several major cities." [24]

The leaders, teachers and students were arrested for supporting the striking workers. Most of those arrested probably ended up in jails, detention camps, or were executed under The Terrorism Act of 1967.

DEMONSTRATORS RETREATING FROM POLICE DOG AFTER ATTEMPTING TO STORM POLICE STATION NEAR CAPE TOWN

Source: *Time,* August 23, 1976, p. 27.

While black and colored South Africans suffer these adversities, whites "live under a hardened shell of comfort, reluctant to awaken to the harsh realities of others like a warm sleeper who does not want to be disturbed." [25] The *New Republic* is therefore quite correct when it says: "Apartheid is not an idiosyncratic, whimsical kind of segregation, but a carefully planned policy of political domination and economic exploitation. The regime still has its crude clowns." [26]

Those "clowns" include high government officials. For example, one government minister, in answer to a white foreign journalist's question, revealed: "We had to detain and ban all these blacks, but we didn't want people to say we are racist, so we threw in a few whites as well." These few whites "thrown in" were most likely thrown out later in secrecy.

DEVASTATION OF SOUTH AFRICAN BLACK FAMILIES

As already noted, millions of blacks are hauled into impoverished homelands. Because of this, the great majority of black breadwinners have to leave their families behind when they leave their "nations" to find work. For this reason many children are deprived of the training offered by both parents, thus making it difficult for such children to be responsible adults of tomorrow. A maid with children, for example, usually leaves the care of her children to her grandmother. The maid is given one day off a month. That is when she sees her children. She has to choose between working to keep her children alive (not in vibrant health) or staying home to train her children and watch them waste away in hunger.

The parents themselves may not have had proper training in the first place, so the undesirable cycle may be passed on from one generation to the next. A migratory lifestyle also makes unity among black South Africans very hard.

Consider the case of a migrant worker reported by the *Progressive*:

Migrant workers, 43 percent of the male force, can *never* qualify for urban residence rights and so must live in dreary single-sex hostels without their families. One couple I met, in which the husband was a migrant worker and father of seven, *had never been able to live together during the entire course of their thirty-one years of marriage.* The wife lived in a "homeland" hundreds of miles away, yet even during her rare visits she could not reside legally with her husband because he lived in a single-sex hostel." [27] (Italics ours).

Since their wedding in 1958, and before he was released from prison on February 11, 1990, Nelson and Winnie Mandela have lived together for only four months!

Unemployed and elderly blacks are repatriated to their "homelands" as "unproductive. "Asian or Colored people have better economic opportunities than the black person and may even be prosperous businessmen, lawyers, or doctors. The lighter the skin, the better the economic opportunities and acceptance. The darker the skin, the worse the economic opportunities and acceptance. While a few blacks may climb the ladder of success, they are so few and far between as to make them almost negligible. Why so? Because of . . .

EDUCATION

The law mandates separate school systems for blacks, Coloreds, Asians, and whites. One color group is prohibited from attending the schools of another color group.

All white children are compelled by law to attend school for at least nine years—from 7 years of age to 16. The Asians and Colored children are also required by law to attend school for eight years—if they live in areas where facilities for attending schools are available. Where they are available, acute shortages of teachers or classrooms are the rule. Only about ten percent of Colored and twenty-five percent of Asian children attend high school.

Black African children are *not* compelled by law to attend school at all, yet many black South African children attend school anyway. Unfortunately, about eighty percent of the black South African children who attend school do not usually complete their primary education (the first six years of schooling). We are not surprised, therefore, that South Africa has a current illiteracy rate of seventy-five percent. Needless to say, the high illiteracy does not portray the true illiteracy rates among South African ethnic groups. Ninety-eight percent of white South Africans are literate, which means that almost seventy-five percent of the illiterate population in South Africa is mainly non-white.

Even those blacks who attend school may be wasting their time. As *Today's Education* of November/December 1980 points out: "According to several experts, the Government's per capita expenditure on Black education is *one-tenth* the expenditure on White education." [28] (Italics ours).

Overcrowding at black schools is common. In some cases, a teacher may be assigned as many as one hundred students per day for a two or three hour session.

Many school buildings are not even fit for education. Take the Crystal High School near Cape Town as an example: "At Crystal, desks were damaged, windows were broken and so many light bulbs were missing that students couldn't read on cloudy days." [29]

Facilities in many black schools are greatly lacking. Compare the facilities in a school in the black South African city of East

FACILITIES IN EAST LONDON HIGH SCHOOL

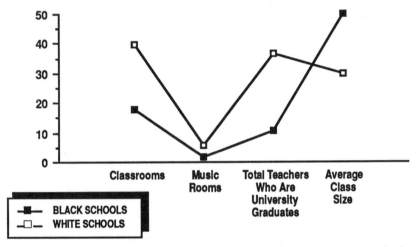

London with those of a high school for whites which served about the same amount of pupils: [30]

"In addition, pupils at the black high school [although poor] must buy workbooks, exercise books, and notebooks, which the white pupils receive free. Similarly, the black school has one overhead projector, whereas the white school has fifteen overhead projectors, six tape recorders, and two film projectors. The white school has subsidized transport and clinic and first aid facilities; the black school has neither.[31]

Out of the sixteen universities in South Africa, eleven are for whites, only three for Africans, one for Asians and one for coloreds. Obviously employment opportunities for educated black South Africans are greatly limited. Lack of sound education greatly hinders South African blacks in many other ways, such as ethnopsychologically. (See chapter ten for further discussion of ethnopsychology). But more importantly, lack of sound education seems to cement white minority rule in South Africa. That is why it has been said that even if apartheid were dismantled today, the road to true equality in South Africa stretches far into the future. The well-educated ones will get the jobs and be the bosses. The less educated (blacks and colored) will have a hard time getting jobs. If he is fortunate enough to land a job, he has a razor-thin margin of ever being the boss. What is more, the economic power is in the hands of whites.

But in the meantime, the pillar of apartheid system has to be smashed, if only on the aspect of recreation.

Racial laws not only govern education, job opportunities, and areas where one can live, but also recreational activities. Beaches, sports facilities, theaters, are all racially segregated. Sports and recreational facilities for non-whites, as in all other things, are inferior to those of whites. Non-whites may not play on white teams, hence the South African Rugby team, the Springbok, which toured a few countries about six years ago, were all whites. Because the all-white rugby team was an unpleasant reminder of racial segregation in South Africa, it was barred from playing in certain countries, including the U.S. and New Zealand.

❖   ❖   ❖

What we have reported is just the tip of the iceberg of atrocities being consistently committed in South Africa. There are many other evils being committed that the South African government does not make known to the public. A South African woman expressed the inhumane treatment of black South Africans succinctly: "If you have sixty eyes, you can't see all the evils of apartheid going on in South Africa." Even if we cannot see all the evils being committed in South Africa, we can be sure of this: the arrests, the brutish treatment, and the blood of men, women and children will continue to flow.

Because the Africans have not been able to free themselves after centuries of abject and bloody domination by the white minority, people have been inclined to believe that the Africans could not help themselves because they were meant to be slaves to whites as a result of the curse by God. Is that so? In view of our discussion up to this point, it is clear that this is not the case. Nonetheless, how do we explain the brutish domination we have been considering? Is not all that an indication of a working curse? We need to answer those questions.

POWER OF CONTROL

There is one important word that explains why the white minority in South Africa dominates the black majority. That word is POWER. Power, according to *Webster* is "ability to compel obedience, control, dominion, prerogative, sovereignty."

Talking about power, the Bible has this to say: "So I returned, and considered all the oppressions that are done under the sun: and behold the tears of such as were oppressed, and they had no comforter; and on the side of their oppressors there was POWER; but they had no comforter" (Ecc. 4:1, AV). "Where the word of a king is, there is POWER: and who may say to him, What doest thou?" (Ecc 8:4, AV).

Here is how two other Bible translations render Ecclesiastes 8:4: "For the King's *word* carries authority. Who can question what he does?" - *The New English Bible*. "Because the word of the king is the *power of control*, and who may say to him, What are you doing?" - *The New World Translations*. (Italics ours).

South African blacks are not the only people ruled by a tyrannical minority, and even commonality of religion among the people living in a country may not be able to restrain the hands of a ruthless ruler. Poland is a case in point.

Ninety-five percent of the Polish people are Catholics. The Catholics, including Pope John Paul II, are vehemently opposed to the Communist regime in Poland. The internationally known Polish trade union called Solidarity is ten million members strong. The trade union, founded and headed by Lech Walesa, is bitterly opposed to the communistic government and has tried its best to topple the regime. Governmental actions from other countries, especially the U.S., have been brought to bear against it. In spite of all that, the communistic rule in Poland survived until recently. Why? Because the rulers, although few in number, have the power of control.

Northern Ireland has not succeeded in seceding from England because England has, as well, the power of control.

The United States government, powerful as it is, was not able to bring General Manuel Noriega of Panama to his knees with economic sanctions. Yet the U.S. has a profound influence on the economy of Panama. And, what is more, the American dollar is the official currency of Panama. The U.S. also stations troops in Panama! Eventually, the U.S. was able to topple Noriega only by invading Panama at a great cost.

Recently, we are all well aware of what happened to Chinese students demanding political reform in China. In spite of the support of Chinese working class and intellectuals, students and their clamor for reform were crushed—literally!

Only a relatively few people rule the Soviet Union: "The privileged political class—the *nomenklatura*—250,000 or so people . . . form the feudal order that dominates the KGB, the military, the

18 million members of the Communistic Party and the masses,"
says *Reader's Digest.* [32]

What, then, about prominent Soviet leaders? "Any leader,"
says the same issue, "will necessarily be bound by and dedicated
to the interests of the *nomenklatura*, since he must have the coop-
eration of its ranks to carry out any program. Khrushchev and, to
an even greater extent, [his successors] were never anything but
the supreme executants of the *nomenklatura*." [33]

The power structure against black South Africans is more
severe than any current communist regime—or any regime for
that matter in the history of Communistic rules. Blacks trying to
free themselves from the police state in South Africa is like a frail
person boxing a giant with copper knuckles.

The Two Key Words Plus One

If a government can succeed in keeping people *illiterate and
poor or economically handicapped,* the controlling power in the
hands of a minority is usually secured. Lack of proper education
acts as a formidable mental handicap in many ways, including the
development of an inferiority complex, passiveness, or an irra-
tionality that can precipitate violence. Emotions may be allowed to
control reasoning instead of reasoning controlling emotions.

Abject poverty, which often affects nutritional balance, can
cause both physical and mental disease. Of course controlling
powers such as judicial, military, and police forces are usually in
the hands of the educated elites.

There is another reason why it is extremely difficult for people
to free themselves from an oppressor: Every effort made by people
to better their lives or liberate themselves is looked upon with the
utmost suspicion, and invariably is ruthlessly crushed. There are
constant house-to-house searches for weapons or anything that
may help people to gain their freedom from the despot who may
be suffering from what is called a "besieged mentality." It is easy,
therefore, to see how people could be controlled, suppressed, and
oppressed.

Blacks Pitted Against Blacks

Reports also show that the South African government sets
blacks against blacks, with the result that blacks slaughter one
another. That kind of insidious tactic is to be expected from the
sort of government whose activities we have been describing. If the
government instigates a black to murder fellow blacks, what further proof is necessary to show that blacks need to be controlled

for their own good? And the government will say, as it has always said, that it needs to take tough actions in order to "maintain law and order." Arrogant, tough talks are backed by brutal actions, but who is really openly and surreptitiously instigating disorder?

Take the case of Ampie Mayisa, the leader of a group opposed to the South African minority regime, as an example. Reports show that Mr. Mayisa was pulled out of his house and hacked to death by pro-government black youths armed with knives, machetes and clubs. He was reported to have been slaughtered in the presence of members of his family. Then his house was fire-bombed.

His twenty-three-year-old son, Joshua Mayisa, said that the apartheid system schemed up the murder of his father and that the system was working hard to "pit black against black and is succeeding." [34]

When the Mayisa family reported the brutal murder to the police, the police said that when the family found the body of their father they should come to the station to report where the body was. The family showed the police the van the attackers used. The van's floor was still drenched with Ampie Mayisa's blood. The police "shrugged."

After a while a group of youths who described themselves as "Concerned Leandra Residents" returned to Mr. Mayisa's house which remains were still smoldering. The youths told reporters that they killed Ampie Mayisa because he was instigating the community, particularly the youth, to enage in an unprovoked clash with the government.

Did the police swoop on the publicly self-confessed murders? Not at all! Instead, who was arrested? Joshua Mayisa, the son of the man who was brutally murdered. And why was he arrested? Because he said to the police officers who came only after the man had been murdered and his house set on fire, "Why weren't you here when my father was being hacked to death?"

The timing of the murder is also crucial. It happened only a few hours before Ampie Mayisa and other anti-apartheid activists were to meet with Chester A. Crocker, the U.S. State Department's top official on African affairs.

Pitting blacks against one another also creates a murderous cycle of revenge, in that one group will want revenge against another group for those murdered. There will hardly be any end to retaliatory actions once it is started. This will not only make the oppressed people look barbaric in the eyes of the world, but also disunites and weakens them.

EFFECTS OF LONG-STANDING OPPRESSION

Furthermore, long-standing oppression can make one act irrationally, out of sheer desperation, especially if one cannot see justice forthcoming. One may be irresistibly urged to take the law into one's own hand. Even a wise or well-educated person may not act judiciously under an oppressive rule, for "surely oppression maketh a wise man mad," says wise King Solomon (Ecc. 7:7, King James). *The New American Bible* says: "For oppression can make a fool of a wise man."

Moreover, wise or educated people may not be able to do much to help the oppressed or themselves under a tyrant, for what people say, their movement and actions are strictly monitored by secret agents. So any efforts people may make to liberate themselves from iron-fisted rulers are crushed before they take root.

A mentally tormenting condition, about which one can do little or nothing, is very harmful to both physical and mental functions. It has been established by physicians that a sustained state of mental torment can cause an abnormal rise in blood pressure, artery malfunction, respiratory problems, liver malfunction, upset the secretion of the gallbladder and the pancreas. Prolonged anger, due either to injustices or other reasons, has been found to have worsened or precipitated such ailments as asthma, eye trouble, skin disease, hives, indigestion, ulcers and even dental trouble. Because of the excessive load rage can put on the body, the body seems to be inflamed. Hence, thinking processes become imbalanced. Rational thinking or forming of logical conclusions becomes extremely difficult. Such conditions can also cause premature old age, usually accompanied by graying of the hair.

Many have to live all their lives under such oppressive or regimented societies. Black South Africans, and others oppressed peoples, fit the conditions we have described. For such, the tendency to strike out could be overwhelming. It has, in fact, been said that many black South Africans walk around like zombies. We are not surprised, therefore, that those oppressed often resort to violence that usually causes destruction of life and property.

At this stage, however, one may say that the 26 million non-white South Africans, literate or not, rich or poor, should be able to unite and help themselves regardless of who has the controlling power. But it is not that simple.

LANGUAGE HANDICAP

The confusion caused by scores of languages spoken in South Africa makes the fight for freedom an uphill battle. To appreciate what we mean, consider that there are more than three hundred Bantu languages in Africa, and at least one hundred of the Bantu languages are spoken in South Africa. Some of the Bantu languages include the following: Swahili, Luba, Kongo, Lingala, Mongo, Ruanda, Rundi, Kikuyi, Kamba, Sukuma, Nyamwezi, Hehe, Chagga, Makonde, Yao, Gisu, Toro, Nyoro, Nyanja, (Chewa) Chiga (Kiga) Tumbuka, Bubki, Mbundu, Tonga, Bemba, Lozi, Ambo and Herero. Additionally, there are the Khoisan languages such as Bushman, Hottentot, Sandawe and Hatsa (Hadzapi). Sandawe can claim about 250,000 speakers, but Hatsa is spoken by a little over 1,000 people.

There are other languages spoken in South Africa, including Afrikaans, Asiatic languages such as Hindustani, and English. Where numerous languages are spoken it is very difficult, even impossible, to unite on anything, obviously including politics. Even in nations where only one language is spoken, politics are chaotic and tangled into the web of the society. And is it not true that political rulers hardly agree unanimously on anything?

True, it is human not to see eye to eye on every issue. But in a polyglot society, prepare for the worst, especially where political issues are involved. That is one of the major reasons why there is so much chaos in South Africa.

It is very important to point out that the languages we mentioned are not dialects any more than the over 1,300 languages spoken in Africa as a whole are dialects. The *Encyclopedia Brittanica* (Vol. 1, 1978) explains: "It is important, when considering the more than 1,000 languages surveyed [in Africa] . . . to emphasize that each language within the subgroup is also important for its own sake. Each language reveals a particular way of communicating about the world, a way that is fully developed and elaborated in its own terms. These languages are certainly not 'undeveloped' or primitive. In fact, the very complexity of analyzing the voltaic languages [or any other group of national languages] in terms of categories sufficiently 'universal' to be operational both for those who already speak the languages and for those who want to learn something about them, reflect their developed nature."

If dialects were to be included in this discussion of language barrier, you can imagine how hopeless the situation could be! Therefore we can understand not only why blacks and whites fight and kill each other, but also why blacks fight among themselves and slaughter one another. Zimbabwe is an example of where blacks slaughtered one another by the thousands in order to free themselves from white domination.

The disagreement among black South Africans about the means they will use to free themselves from a white minority domination is not peculiar to them. Such disunity, and consequent slaughtering of one another, is to be found in many parts of the world. Northern Ireland, Nicaragua, Argentina and Lebanon are a few examples.

Although currently most South African whites are at peace with one another, it has not always been that way. Take the Anglo-Boer war of 1899 as an example. The conflict between the Dutch and English descendants of South Africans lasted four years at a cost of over 40,000 lives.

We do not want to get the idea that languages can cause problems only in underdeveloped countries or among a color group of people who are said to be cursed. They can cause untold problems and damages in developed countries too.

DEVELOPED NATIONS AND LANGUAGE PROBLEMS

Among developed countries, Canada furnishes a classic example. Although only two main languages, English and French, are spoken in Canada, centuries-old chaos still exists among English- and French-speaking Canadians. At one time French- speaking Canadians threatened to secede from English-speaking Canadians. Even now it does not seem that the political problems between the two factions are lying in the casket.

During the American Revolutionary War, one-third of the Americans were in favor of liberating themselves from British rule, one-third were against self-rule, and the last one-third did not care a bit who ruled them. The Americans who were in favor of British rule were known as the Tories. Believe it or not, members of the Tory Party fought alongside the British soldiers so that the U.S. would remain under British domination. What was wrong? Did they forget the reason why the pilgrim fathers left Britain? Now, those who were for, against, or neutral in the conflict spoke the same language! What would you have expected if they spoke more than one hundred tribal languages!

Even today, some in the U.S. would still prefer British rule to Americans ruling America. "That's pushing it too far," you may say. Seems so, but if there are Americans who prefer Nazi or Communist rule to the present system of ruling in the U.S., should anyone be surprised if some still prefer to be ruled by the British or other forms of government?

Can you think of a single problem, however simple, however obvious the solution may seem to be, however pressing the need to solve it, about which there is a consensus of opinion on how the problem should be solved?

Take South Africa itself as an example. Not all white South Africans are in favor of white minority rule, and some of them would not mind overthrowing the present regime. Indeed, many white South Africans are living in political asylum in other countries, or are in jail, or were killed for siding with blacks as regards apartheid. On the other hand, if blacks were ruling South Africa, and whites were fighting for their freedom from black domination, some blacks would side with the whites. In fact, many South African blacks have been killed by blacks on the accusation of spying for the South African white regime.

Perhaps this is the greatest irony of it all. During the time the abolition of slavery in the United States was a hot political issue, whites living in Southern States inducted black slaves into their armies. The blacks were used to fight the U.S. Federal Government which was trying to abolish slavery. Such black slave soldiers were like a turkey fighting against the abolition of Thanksgiving or Christmas!

DEVELOPED NATIONS AND TRIBAL INSTINCT

You may recall that we mentioned in chapter one that some people think that tribalism being practiced in Africa may be because the black people were cursed. Tribalism is not as a result of a curse. Language is the chief reason why tribalism is practiced in many parts of the world, especially in Asia and Africa. People gravitate to those who speak the same language, and thus tribalism was born. Therefore, the chaos, hostilities and bloodshedding tribalism often causes cannot be attributed to a curse.

Citizens of developed nations will tribalize if several native languages are spoken in such societies. Canada has been cited as an example of a long-standing cultural problem between English and French Canadians. If 50 native languages—a language to each state—were spoken in the U.S., can you imagine how easy it would be to practice tribalism among U.S. citizens?

In a weekly news event roundtable such as ABC's "This Week with David Brinkley," how often do the commentators agree on the method in which the issues aired should be solved? Now, let us assume that the three commentators and David Brinkley himself spoke four tribal languages! The confusion that may ensue from language confusion and accusations of favoritism among the four imagined language groups may make airing the program prohibitive. And, although only one dominant language is spoken in the U.S., is it not true that each state (sometimes each city) fights for its own welfare, even at the expense of other states or cities?

The language situation in the areas of the world where tribalism is practiced is much worse than the way we used the U.S. as an illustration. Take the Ivory Coast in West Africa as an example. Its land area is smaller than the state of California, with a population of a little more than nine million (according to 1984 census), compared to California's almost 24 million (1980 census). But more than sixty languages are spoken in Ivory Coast!

Let us use sporting events to show that people living in developed countries are walking a fine edge of tribalistic instinct. When soccer and American football are played, the audience usually roots for the team from their home state, city or town. In the absence of a team from their home state, city or town, their favorite team is supported. Let us now assume that their favorite team speaks a different language from that of the opposing team. Do you think that, in such a situation, people will tribalize? Yes, indeed! They have already unmistakably displayed tribal instincts by rooting for the team of their choice. Also, as fanatic fans pull for their home team, and boo and recklessly adjectivize the opposing team with unsavory words, phrases and physical gestures, a melee that could result in serious injuries or even death may ensue. The situation just described is true of many soccer events in some parts of the world, but especially in South America, and lately in Europe. And in most fist-fighting soccer events in South America, both teams speak the same language!

Really, then, tribalism is practiced worldwide, but the practice of tribalism is more profound and destructive in the polyglot societies of Africa, parts of Asia and Central America than in societies not language-bewildering.

While tribalism has its own inherent evils, the root of racism in South Africa goes a little deeper than that.

ROOT OF RACISM IN SOUTH AFRICA

It is said that "there are at least 4,000 churches and sects in South Africa alone, which claim to be very religious!" And over 83 percent of both white and black South Africans, who claim to be Christians, belong to those churches. Undoubtedly, many whites who practice racial discrimination and engage in inhumane acts, such as we have been discussing, are members of those churches and sects! In fact, the Dutch Reformed Church was responsible for the apartheid law in South Africa. The Church used the Bible (especially Genesis 9:20-27 we quoted in chapter three) to support racial separation in South Africa. Police have actually been reported as saying to blacks, "I arrest you in the name of God." Do they also shoot and kill them in the name of God? So, the Church has, by implication, made God an accomplice of its racism and the accompanied bloodshed! Can a church be more guilty of sacrilege and inhumane acts?

One wonders how those who claim to worship God can sponsor, enact, support and enforce with relentless brutality laws bent upon destroying fellow humans physically, mentally and morally. How can such ones dare preach the love of fellow humans in their religious buildings, and in their homes pray to God and eagerly look forward to going to heaven without being tugged by their consciences? Will there be color lines in heaven?

In view of our discussions in this chapter, we can clearly see why it is very difficult for black South Africans to raise their heads from the relentless oppression of the iron-fisted rulers. What, though, do we say about blacks who are given *equal educational and occupational opportunities as whites and other colors?* Yet it seems that blacks still do not generally measure up. Therefore, many people seem to have reasons to reinforce the belief that blacks are inferior to whites, or cursed, or even suffer from both curse and mental inferiority. That subject will be taken up next, and you may find that there is much more to the matter than is generally known.

NOTES

1. Population figures are based on 1984 census.

2. Transkei, the homeland of Xhosa people, was granted independence by the South African government in October, 1976. The land they occupy was allocated to them by the South African government. Most of the Transkei's land is hilly, mountainous, dry and dull. Other so-called black independent states include Bophuthatswana and Venda. Only South African government recognized those arid homelands and forced settlements as independent states.

3. "Black Rage In South Africa," *New Republic,* 20 July 1976, p. 9.

4. "A Tragic Turn to Terrorism," *Newsweek,* 10 Oct. 1977, p. 51.

5. "Pretoria Doctor Loses License," *New York Times,* 17 Oct. 1985, p. 7.

6. Afrikaans is the language developed by people of European descent who settled in South Africa. These people are called Afrikaners. Although Germanic in structure and vocabulary, Africaans is a conglomeration of Dutch, Flemish, English, French, and Hottentot.

7. "After Soweto, Anger and Unease," *Time,* 5 July, 1976, p. 40.

8. "Crimes Against Southern African Women, Children," *U.N. Chronicle,* July, 1980, p. 12.

9. "Cape Towns Bloody Boycott," *Newsweek,* 9 June, 1980, p. 59.

10. "Johannesburg Diarist," *New Republic,* 19 July, 1980, p. 39.

11. Edward A. Gargam. "U.S. Group Charges Wide Beating of Children By South Africa Police," *New York Times,* 18 April, 1986, p. A4.

12. "South African Police Accused of Child Torture, Killing," *Los Angeles Times,* 18 April 1986, p. 9.

13. "Apartheid in Action," *Ms. Magazine,* Oct., 1976, p. 58.

14. The "Pass Law" has now been repealed after 25 years of operation, but the repealing of the law has not changed the basic foundation of apartheid.

15. "Black Education in South Africa," *Today's Education,* Nov./Dec., 1980, p. 56.

16. "Terror and Repression," *Time,* 31 Aug. 1981, p. 31.

17. According to recent reports, that number has doubled since 1980.

18. "Johannesburg Diatrist," *New Republic,* 19 July 1980, p. 39.

19. "Megan Adams, "A Bitter Season in South Africa," *Progressive,* June, 1980, Vol. 44, No. 6, p. 51.

20. Indres Naidoo, *Robben Island,* (New York, Vintage Books, 1983), p. 68.

21. "A Bitter Season in South Africa,"' *Progressive,* June, 1980, p. 54.

22. Ibid., p. 55.

23. *Concept of Race,* p. 258.

24. Peter Younghusband, "Cape Town's Bloody Boycott," Newsweek, 9 June, 1980, p. 59.

25. "A Bitter Season in South Africa," Progressive, June, 1980, p. 55.

26. James North, "Johannesburg Diarist," New Republic, July 19, 1980, p. 39.

27. "A Bitter Season in South Africa," *Progressive,* June, 1980, p. 51.

28. *Today's Education,* Nov./Dec., p. 58.

29. Ibid., p. 59.

30. Ibid., p. 59.

31. Ibid., p. 59.

32. John Barron, "Who Really Rules Russia?" *Readers Digest,* Vol. 127, No. 759, July, 1985, p. 114.

33. Ibid., p. 114.

34. "Black Slain on the Eve of U.S. Official Visit," *Los Angeles Times,* 13 January, 1986, p. 16.

NINE

AMERICANS THAT ARE
NEARLY NOT AMERICANS

"We hold these truths to be self-evident, that all men are created equal, that they are endowed by their Creator with certain inalienable Rights, that among these are Life, Liberty and the pursuit of Happiness."

That quotation, chiefly written by Thomas Jefferson, is part of the United States Declaration of Independence. The Declaration, adopted on July 4, 1776, is believed to be one of the most important state papers in American history, second only to the Federal Constitution of 1787.

However, for many Americans, especially blacks, that Declaration of Independence was true only on paper and not in spoken words and deeds. It is common knowledge that black Americans have been treated with contempt and hatred, yet the United States champions human rights and spares no castigative words or punitive actions against other nations guilty of the violation of human rights.

Who does not know that "the Southern States regarded slaves not as persons, but as property and enacted legislation to assure the stability of the slave regime and the complete subordination of the slave population. Slaves could not own property, possess firearms, engage in commerce, leave the plantation without the permission of their owners, testify in court except against other Negroes, make contracts, *learn to read and write*, or hold meetings without the presence of white persons. They were prohibited from striking white persons, but the murder or rape of a slave or a free Negro by a white person was not regarded as a serious offense." - *Encyclopedia Americana* (Vol. 20, 1987). (Italics ours).

Although intermarriage was prohibited in all Southern states (as well as in many northern and western states), and cohabitation of black men with white resulted in horrendous punishment for the black male, the sexual exploitation of Negro women by white men was tolerated.

About the sexual exploitation of blacks, Dr. Manning Marable, political economist at Cornell University's African Studies Center, said:

> Historian Winthrop Jordan argues that the threat of black slave revolts in the seventeenth and eighteenth centuries was usually perceived in sexual terms. The notion existed that black men were particularly virile, promiscuous and lusted after white women. It is apparent that white men projected their own desire onto Negroes: their own passion for black women was not fully acceptable to society or the self and hence not readily admissible. Black women, however, were held to be naturally lascivious and passionate, and thus fair game for sexual predation. The sexual pathology of whites was enshrined as public policy in laws permitting castration of blacks. In colony after colony, from Quaker to Pennsylvania to the Carolinas, castration became a form of legal punishment for a whole set of black male offenses.[1]

BRED FOR SALE

Slaves were bred for sale as if they were domestic animals. Families were broken by selling parents separately from their children. Unable to withstand the strain of self-degradation or cruel treatment, many slaves committed suicide, mutilated themselves or, where they could, killed their owners. Those who killed their owners, if caught, were destroyed.

Life after the Civil War did not improve much for blacks. Lynchings, for example, took place at an average rate of 166 annually for blacks from 1890 to 1900. Summary executions were either by hanging, shooting or burning. After 1900, lynchings decreased. For example, only seventy blacks were executed arbitrarily in 1919.

BLACK AMERICANS' SOCIAL STATUS

Where they were rated at all, blacks were regarded as second-class citizens and given second-class treatment and opportunities, such as second-class schooling. They were restricted from certain

The weeping ghosts of slaves kept cold and shackled in the attic appear at the Old Slave House in Illinois. It stands one mile south of the intersections of Highways 1 and 13 on the Kentucky border. *(The Bettmann Archive.)*

In the Draft Riots of 1863, mobs attacked at random, and rioters pursued and killed fleeing blacks in New York City. *(Museum of the City of New York.)*

types of employment and many other opportunities enjoyed by whites. Many whites, especially in the northern states, refused to work side by side with blacks. Blacks were barred from hotels, motels, restaurants, and public transportation used by whites. Where they were allowed to eat in public places, they had a spe-

Indiana was the scene of these lynchings, which took place in the 1920s. *(Library of Congress.)*

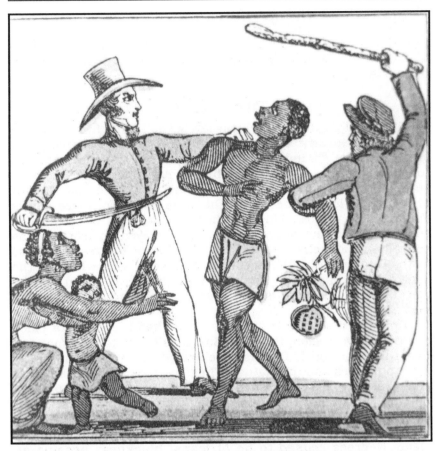

West Indies Slave traders cruelly beat up Negro and separate him from his family. The Black Man's Lament. *(The Bettmann Archive.)*

cial secluded area (usually at the back of the kitchen), where they could eat without being seen by the public. They were not allowed seats in movie theaters. In order to watch a movie, they had to come early and stay in the balcony. Blacks were also banned from libraries, barber shops, and public parks. Any blacks who challenged these restrictions were either publicly whipped, imprisoned, summarily executed or punished in other ways. If a black man tried on a suit or a hat in a store, he had to buy it. After all, who would want to buy an article a black person had fitted himself into!

Concerning the attitude of many American whites toward

black Americans, the *New Catholic Encyclopedia* (Vol. 3, 1967), has this to say: "Only in the United States were slaveholders convinced that the difference between Negroes and whites was so fundamental that the black man could never be regarded as anything but a slave."

FREED SLAVES THAT ARE NOT TRULY FREE!

When talking about black slavery in the United States, are we dealing with ancient history of, say, two or three hundred years ago? No, not at all. Indeed the grandparents of many living blacks today were slaves. Alas, many blacks not much older than 60 years remember not being able to try on a hat or a suit without buying it. As late as the 1950s, the mass media portrayed blacks as inferior to whites. Generally their role was that of servants to whites. Even today many blacks are portrayed on television as servants, maids, chauffeurs, cooks, waiters or waitresses and so forth. Undoubtedly, the social lot of blacks as a whole in the United States has greatly improved from those bygone but not forgotten days, yet there is still a great deal more to be accomplished.

However, it seems certain that a mold had been cast for black Americans even before they were taken as slaves to the Americas. Regarding the mold, Dr. Marable said, "The transformation of African peoples into the status of 'Negroes' took place *before* black chattel slavery was established as the dominant means of production in the Southern United States . . . Blacks alone were set apart because of their skin color. And as early as 1660 in the Virginia colony, blackness itself was identical with the status of a chattel slave. Negroes *ceased* to be Africans; blackness became an ascribed status rising out of whites' demands for black labor, rather than a distinctive culture or even a condition of humanity." [2] (Italics ours.)

A brief look at the history of slavery confirms what Dr. Marable said.

AFRICAN SLAVERY

Encyclopedia Britannica (Vol. 15, p. 862, 1978), estimated that about 15 million African slaves were shipped across the Atlantic. The manner in which the slaves were transported was more than barbaric: men and women alike were transported naked; their heads were shaved and branded to identify their owners. They were made to sit in the hold of the ship, packed so tightly that they were sitting on each other's laps. Then they were secured by leg-irons so that movement became extremely difficult and painful. If the ship's hold was full, slaves were usually secured on the deck. Yet it took months for a ship to traverse the Atlantic from Africa to America.

Due to the brutish way of transporting slaves, incredible numbers died before reaching their destinations. For example, in 1829, only 481 of the 800 slaves that left a Portuguese port in

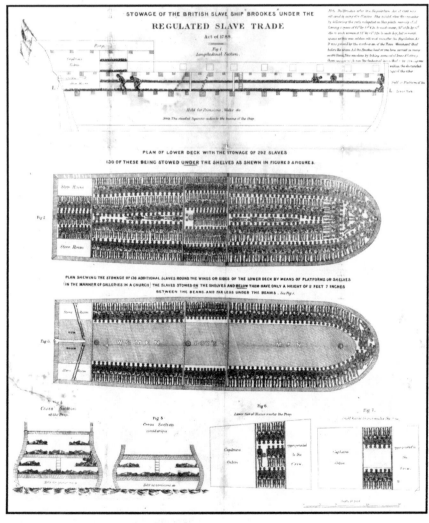

Slaves packed like sardines. *(Library of Congress.)*

Billboard announces a
"raffle," at which the
prize is a mulatto girl.
*(The Granger
Collection.)*

In a typical pre-Civil war slave auction, "merchancise" went to the highest bidder.
(The Granger Collection.)

Mozambique made it alive to their destination. Those who died were dumped into the ocean. It has been said that at least twenty percent of the slaves shipped from Africa died aboard ship. This means that 3 million Africans perished and were dumped into the ocean.

Encyclopedia of Black America says: "It is said that sharks often followed slave ships, feeding upon bodies that were sure to be tossed overboard." [3]

Upon arriving at their destinations, slaves were caged like wild beasts before being auctioned. To prevent rebellion, families were separated, given different names, and sold individually to different owners.

FIRST APPEARANCE OF SLAVES IN THE UNITED STATES

In the year 1619 the first twenty African slaves arrived in North America. They were transported by a Dutch ship to Jamestown, Virginia. Daubed "indentured servants" [4] at first, their roles and title quickly changed from that of servants to that of abused slaves. The twenty blacks were the beginning of the massive slave trade. By the late 1600s slavery was well established in North America, and slaves numbered in the millions. By 1860, there were 4,441,830 black slaves in the United States. Out of that number, only 448,070 were considered free. Even those that were considered free either bought their freedom or ran away from their masters. Furthermore, they were free only in words but not socially and economically, as we will discuss later. Slaves were treated as inferior, as a cursed species of humans. Some even regarded them as beasts, as we have noted in chapter one.

That blacks were treated as inferior to whites was confirmed by visitors to the United States. One such visitor was William Chambers, an English traveler in the U.S. in 1855. He was quoted as having observed: "There seems, in short, to be a fixed notion throughout the whole of the States, whether slave or free, that colored is by nature a subordinate race and that, in no circumstances, can it be considered equal to the white." [5]

Speaking for those who approved of the slave trade, Thomas Cooper of South Carolina said: "We talk a great deal of nonsense about the rights of man. We say that man is born free, and equal to every other man. Nothing can be more untrue: no human being ever was, now is or ever will be born free." [6]

The notion that blacks were inferior and so needed to be treated differently was also manifested in the kinds of jobs the majority of them held, even after slavery was abolished, if they were not denied employment altogether.

BLACK AMERICANS AND EMPLOYMENT OPPORTUNITIES

Joblessness or menial jobs is an established tradition among many blacks in the United States, Britain and South Africa. About blacks in the U.S. we are informed: "Fortified with an ideology of racial inferiority of Negroes (and of 'white supremacy'), the dominant group felt justified in its limitation, or total denial, of basic human and citizenship rights to Negroes. Economically the vast majority of Negroes were poor agricultural tenants, mostly share-croppers or laborers in the web of the plantation system. The substantial number of Negro artisans and skilled workers at the close of the Civil War in 1865 declined consistently as white laborers and trade unions effectively excluded Negroes and prevented them from learning trades, thus forcing them into unskilled and agricultural work." (*Encyclopedia Americana*, Vol. 20, 1979).

Looking at the present economic status of black Americans, what do we find? Black unemployment is two and one-half times that of white workers. Unemployment among black youths is thirty-eight to forty percent. and up to sixty percent in some big cities. It is even worse than that in some big-city ghettos.

U.S. News & World Report of June 2, 1980 reported: "For black teenagers in some big-city ghettos, the jobless rate approaches 80 percent, official estimates." These unemployment figures swing up and down in response to the state of the nation's economy.

On the other hand, unemployment among white youths was at a mere six percent in 1978. That six percent unemployment for white youths could have been even lower if they had been willing to take any jobs that came their way.

Many blacks have tried so hard and unsuccessfully to secure employment that they could be dubbed professional job seekers. Youths, usually full of energy, do not know what to do with themselves. Consequently, in utter frustration, they resort to lives of criminality, immorality or vandalism. Those who are unable to stand the strain of a life of perennial frustration and worthlessness commit suicide. Suicide rates among young black Americans are on the increase.

When blacks do get jobs, they are usually the last to be hired and the first to be fired. Most blacks, therefore, seem to be in a permanent depression. A national economic slump drives the black unemployment figure, already intolerably high, even higher. Prolonged joblessness causes frustration and destroys self-confidence, especially when one is powerless to do anything about it. This is partly why riots periodically devastate many big cities of the United States and Britain. As a result of prolonged jobless-ness, many blacks have lost the will to work and have become psychologically shattered. They are suffering from ergasiopho-bia—the fear of work. This kind of attitude is not unnatural. It is called "inertia," but we can call it "body inertia." It is a condition where one abhors a change once one has trained one's body in a particular way. As an example, if you are used to working all your life, or if you drink or smoke, or engage in any other activities reg-ularly, the deprivation of any of those things may lead to nervous-ness and restlessness. Those who are used to exercising usually feel like engaging in it, rain or shine, but as for prolonged jobless-ness, the body conditions itself to idleness. That is why some blacks may decline a job when offered, or may not perform up to par. Gradual introduction to work seems to be the best way to solve such a problem. But who, in this day and time, can afford the luxury of gradually introducing somebody to working habits?

The unemployment picture among British blacks is not any better. One of the main reasons attributed to recent riots which ravaged Britain was unemployment. The American sociologist, Nathan Glazer, believes that the British riots are much in the mold of American race riots of the 1960s.

According to Glazer, "What you have is a group of people who have full legal rights as citizens, yet are deprived of all social and economic participation in the society. This is a version of the American dilemma: blacks had full legal status but not full eco-nomic status." [7] The same magazine continues: "But other experts, and blacks themselves, felt that racial discrimination was a significant factor. 'As soon as I come in for a job interview,' says a young black woman, 'it's no.' " [8]

For example, unemployment among blacks in general in Britain in 1981 was forty percent, but sixty percent among British black youths. Alex Bennett, a community relations worker in Toxteth said: "Black men between the ages of 17 and 28 in Liverpool may never have worked a day in their lives. Is it any sur-prise that they are tremendously resentful?" [9]

No wonder that a black employment counselor said: "My advice to my kid is, 'Get on at school, and get out of Liverpool, because there is nothing here for you.'" Another black who has been looking for a job for four years commented: "There is nothing here for us." [10]

It is now believed that discrimination in employment against British blacks is increasing. Reported the *Newsweek* of July 27, 1981: "A government report released last week noted an alarming rate in racial harassment and violence, and said discrimination in employment might actually be increasing." [11] In the township of Southhall, for example, all its entire 120-person police force is white, yet about half of the residents of Southhall are non-white. Only one-half of one percent of the police force in London Metropolitan is non-white. That translates to only about 119 non-white police officers out of 22,369 policemen, yet London is a multiracial city with large populations of blacks and Asians.

It is bad enough not to have a job, but devastating to be refused the opportunity to make a living because of the color of one's skin. Those who have never been without a job—or have never been refused a job because of their color—may not quite realize how a life without work and hope can demoralize a person. The economic depression of 1929-1935 showed in graphic ways how a gloomy outlook can affect one's life. When people lost their jobs or businesses, many became ill and never recovered. Other abandoned their children or committed suicide. Those who were not too proud, or accepted things as they came, lined up for food and other kinds of handouts. It does not seem difficult, therefore, to imagine how gloomy life must be for people who have been in an economically depressed state most of their lives, or refused jobs because of the color of their skin, while others enjoyed economic boom.

BLACKS AND POVERTY

Abject poverty is usually an inevitable consequence of joblessness. Since high unemployment is a tradition among blacks, wretched poverty also becomes a way of life for most of them. For example, according to the U. S. Census Bureau, among almost 25 million people considered poor in the United States in 1978, over thirty-one percent of them were blacks; around twenty-two percent were of "Hispanic origin." That means that around eight million of about 20 million blacks in the United States are poor! Whereas only nine percent of the poor were white.

USA Today confirmed black American poverty: "Median black family income is only 57 percent that of whites—lower than it was in 1966!" [12] The *New York Times* testified: "In the last decade (1970-1980), real income for the median white family increased by less than 1 percent, to $21,904, but real income for the median black family decreased 5 percent, to $12,674." [13]

You may, at this stage, wonder about all the legislative efforts, such as "Affirmative Action" or "Operation Push," geared to improve the lot of blacks in the United States. Are they working?

The *New York Times Magazine* of October 5, 1980 reported: "More than a decade has passed since the nation established new laws aimed at correcting the civil wrongs that held most of black America in thrall. Yet despite these legal gains, and a significant change in public attitudes that made it easier for blacks to enter society's mainstream, a disheartening number of black men, women and children remain in the closed world of poverty and despair." [14]

Vernon E. Jordan, president of the National Urban League, was quite right when he said, "It is clear that, for all the progress some blacks have made, half of all black Americans are boat people without boats, cast adrift in a hostile ocean of discrimination, unemployment, and poverty.

"It is clear that black progress has been limited. It is clear that blacks remain disadvantaged. It is clear that race continues to be a major determining factor in our society." [15]

The impoverished conditions apply with equal force to British blacks since they are in the same economic, social and racial bind as black Americans. And, as has been discussed in the previous chapter, the lot of South African blacks is incomparably worse than that of either British or American blacks.

HIGH MINORITY PRISON POPULATION IN U.S. JAILS

The prison population in the United States contains all colors. However, black Americans make up a more than proportionate share of the inmates. *Encyclopedia Americana* (Vol. 22, 1978), hammered the nail on the head: "But the fact is that the more enlightened the judicial policy is, the rougher and more depressing is the profile of the prisoner who is finally precipitated into the prison. With few exceptions the record reveals: male, urban, low education, high unemployment, previous conviction for crime. Near metropolitan centers, almost 75 percent of the new arrivals are black or Hispanic."

It is obvious, therefore, that many who have been imprisoned or are behind bars today would not be there if they were not "precipitated" by such things as joblessness, abject poverty and "low education" to commit crimes. So the inequality and discriminatory attitude in society could be blamed for the high percentage of minority population in the prison yards of the United States, and, indeed, of other countries, especially South Africa.

Adding to their problem is the environment in the prison. Regarding these conditions, the same Encyclopedia informs: "The prison is a ghetto for its inmates. Within its walls it confines, houses, feeds, clothes, educates, and polices its population. It compresses into its miniscule territory many of the tormenting problems of an urban society: overcrowding, poverty, violence, racial friction, and a pervasive sense of alienation and despair. Within such a setting, is there a possibility of rehabilitation for prison?"

The prison grounds themselves are the sum total of the environment the prisoner left behind, except that they are even more highly concentrated and frustrating, vicious and dangerous. The prison grounds then become an advanced training school in crime for those who are not yet hardened criminals. We can therefore see why crimes flourish.

Once they have served their terms in jail, their lives do not generally improve, simply because they usually return to the conditions they were in before going to jail. Finding decent employment is often more difficult with a prison record. So out of bitterness, or sheer frustration, or just to meet the bare necessities of life, many resort to a life of criminality. For these reasons prison population has a good percentage of people who have been convicted before.

There are other reasons why minorities in the United States make up a large percentage of the prison population. Let us listen to *The Nation* of April 11, 1981: "In all racist states blacks make up a disproportionately large percentage of the prison population compared with their numbers in the society as a whole. In the United States, studies have shown that black, Hispanic and poor defendants are the ones who receive harsher sentences and more meager legal services than middle-class whites who commit identical crimes." [16]

The nationwide statistics compiled by the University of Iowa law professor, David Baldus, show that race plays an important factor in handing down death sentences. Reporting about the survey, *The Los Angeles Times* of April 23, 1987, says a study showed that "murderers were eleven times more likely to receive the death sentence if the victim was white rather than black." But what of when the killer was white? In "eight percent of the cases" the death sentence was handed down. What if the killer was black? In "twenty-two percent of" the cases, the death sentence was pronounced.

Take Georgia as an example. The same *Los Angeles Times* reports that "the majority of murder victims in Georgia are black, but none of their killers has been executed." But "six blacks who killed whites and one white whose victim is white have been executed." A TV commentator interpretated such discrepancies in death sentences to mean that those who decide the fate of a guilty person are saying that the life of a white person is more precious than the life of a black person.

VIOLENT DEATHS AND COLOR GROUPS

Moreover, the number of blacks and persons of other minority groups who die violent deaths that are not accident related are disproportionately higher than whites who die violent deaths. Let us consider some examples, using homicidal figures for males first. (Death rates are per 100,000 population.) In 1960, 3.6 whites died violent deaths; 34.5 blacks and other colors died of the same cause in the same year; 6.8 whites died of homicide in 1970, whereas 60.8 blacks and other colors died in the same year through the same cause; 62.6 blacks and others died of homicide in 1970 and 9.1 whites died in the same year from the same cause. The figures among white females and black females and other females are also disproportionately high. For example, in 1977, homicide among white females was 2.9 per 100,000 population; whereas in the same year it was 12.0 among black females and other colors. [17]

It seems that many have been forced into a life of criminality that culminated in violent death. Admittedly, there are those who would prefer a life of criminality to honest living and who will not change regardless of what is done for them, or to them. For "though the wicked should be shown favor, he simply will not learn righteousness. In the land of straightforwardness he will act unjustly" (Isa. 26:10; NW). And "even if you should pound the foolish one with a pestle in a mortar, in among cracked grain, his foolishness will not depart from him" (Pro. 27:22 NW).

However, is it not equally likely that many of those who appear to be habitual criminals today might be saved if suitable employment were provided? Who or what provides employment? Of course, the society. If those qualified and willing to work are deliberately denied jobs, who is to be blamed for the crimes that may be committed out of frustration or just to stay alive? You guessed right—the society. And who or what really suffers? The society, of course. And in many ways. For one thing, the "have nots" usually steal from those who have. The well-to-do, therefore, often live a life of fear, not only of being robbed, which happens often, but of being hurt or killed. Many who have plenty cannot enjoy their abundance in peace, while those who do not have are not in peace because they lack the necessities of life.

Furthermore, the society pays to maintain the jails in which criminals are housed only to be let loose and become menaces to the society again, and then probably return to jail once more. So the vicious cycle continues.

You may be saying to yourself that you have met many black Americans whose performance on the job is below par when compared to other colors. Is that not good reason to refuse them a job? Must their low performance on the job be attributed to a curse or to inferiority?

NUTRITION AND JOB PERFORMANCE

It is a solidly established fact that poor nutrition can inflict a permanent blow to the brain. How do black Americans and other poor Americans fit into this situation? Many black American children lacked proper nourishment in their development from infancy to adulthood, and we are not talking about a long time ago.

As late as the 1960s, a United States Congressional Investigation found black children starving, weakened, listless, or dying for lack of nourishment (not to say *proper* nourishment), especially in the Southern states, and particularly in Mississippi. Those children are the young adults of today who are probably among the 38-40 percent unemployed, or among the 60 percent unemployed in some big cities. And those who, by a stroke of fortune, secure a job may not be able to perform up to par simply because of malnutrition as a child.

Concerning the part which a balanced diet plays in the mental and physical functions of people, Dr. Robert S. Goodhart and Associate Professor of Medicine of Cornell University Medical College and Dr. Maurice E. Shills, experts in the field, state in their book, *Modern Nutrition in Health and Disease*: "A decreased intake (of food) for age, even when it could be fairly satisfactory for size *perpetuates* undernutrition." [18] They also mentioned in the same book that nutrition has an effect on "psychomotor," or conscious mental activity as well as "mental development." We can expect then that starving children in the U.S. and the world as a whole have sustained a permanent mental blow because of lack of proper nutrition.

Echoing the same opinion, Professor Montagu says:

But if *nutrition is poor*, health care deficient, housing debasing, family income low, family disorganization prevalent, discipline anarchic, ghettoization more or less complete, personal worth consistently diminished, expectations low, and aspirations frustrated, as well as numerous other environmental handicaps, then one may expect the kind of

*failures in intellectual development that are so often gratu-
itously attributed to genetic factors.* Those who make such
attributions fail to understand how dependent the development of intelligence is upon the reduction of such conditions of privations, frustration, and hopelessness.[19]

The condition described not only causes brain damage, but
brain damage in turn affects one's general attitude in almost all
facets of life, as well as affecting children yet to be fathered. Again,
Professor Montagu concurred with this:

There is a class of brain damage of sociogenic origin to
which, it seems to me, insufficient attention has been paid.
Functional expressions of this class of brain damage are
the deficits of behavior, and especially in motivation, learning ability, and *intelligence which are produced by malnutrition.*

It is generally agreed that the most important factor in
the healthy development of the *conceptus is nutrition*—not
merely nutrition of the mother's mother, and probably also
of the mother's father, not to mention the child's own
father.[20] (Italics ours.)

It should be pointed out that sociogenic brain damage can be
completely reversed under improved environmental conditions.
However, such adverse environmental conditions do cause, in an
infant, generally imperceptible mental damage, usually before the
age of three years when the brain has already attained four-fifths
of its maximum adult size. Child psychologists believe that the
first three years of a child's environment and training has an
inerasable impact on him for the rest of his life. In view of what
Dr. Montagu said, it is quite possible that the baby has been
adversely affected emotionally and mentally before birth. Many
black Americans fit the conditions described above.

BLACK NEIGHBORHOODS

Many people say that black neighborhoods are not properly
taken care of, or that when they move into another neighborhood,
property depreciates, illegitimacy goes up, drugs are pushed, rob-
bery and other crimes increase. Therefore, people try to avoid
them as neighbors or move away from them. For the love of good
and a sense of decency, it is natural for people to condemn those
practices. It is also easy to say that it doesn't cost much to keep
one's home clean, and water the lawn, and that it is difficult to

understand why people wallow in filth instead of doing something to help themselves. After all, they have all the time in the world.

But that is not the way things work. When people are not happy, they hardly do anything to help themselves. We have all been depressed one time or another. Can you remember the last time you were "down in the dumps," as they say? You had no money or job, and the hope of getting a job was dim indeed. Did you, at such a time, happily spend time cleaning your house, mowing and watering the lawn? Some in such conditions have taken their lives and sometimes those of others. On the other hand, when you had money or a good job, did you take good care of your home and yourself? Most likely. Really, then, when people are without jobs and hope, and know that the society does not welcome them, they let go the upkeep of their homes and bodies, and also destroy their neighborhood as a way of venting their anger against the society.

We can see, then, why black neighborhoods may not be well cared for. That society contributes to the deterioration of black neighborhoods was confirmed by the *New York Times Magazine*:

> Yet, in spite of the very real gains, the goal of unqualified racial equality has remained tantalizingly elusive.
>
> As the more blatant forms of racial segregation, rejection and cruelty decreased in the Southern states, the predicament of blacks confined to the Northern urban ghettos worsened. As segregation was eliminated at Southern and border states, residential segregation remained fixed and the number of segregated schools increased in Northern cities. [21]

EDUCATION, PROFESSIONAL FIELDS AND BLACK AMERICANS

A school child who is not wholly accepted in the community or not provided the opportunity for better education is likely to fare badly in a world where some form of education is a prerequisite to doing almost anything. If such a situation is sustained and intensified for a long period of time against a person or a group of people, the effects could be demoralizing and dehumanizing. Many black Americans have found themselves in this situation.

You may recall that we made a reference to the fact that it was unlawful at one time for black Americans to "learn to read and write." Even when it was no longer a violation of the law for blacks to be educated, what was the quality of education they received? According to the *Encyclopedia Americana* (Vol. 20, 1979):

The dual system in education which became universal marked from the beginning a wide disparity in support of Negro education from public funds. The inadequacy of public funds for education generally prompted a reduction in per capita expenditures for Negro children as the only means of enlarging the per capita expenditures for white children, and even then the expenditures [for Negro children before the Negro children's educational funds were diverted to educate white children] were far below the average for the rest of the country.

The [segregated] Negro schools have felt this disparity in fewer and underpaid teachers, poorer school buildings and equipment, shorter school terms, and ultimately, lower literacy and educational achievement on the part of Negroes.

THE FIRST BLACK AMERICAN COLLEGE GRADUATE

It took over two hundred years for black Americans to produce a college educated person. John Russwurm was the first black American college graduate. From 1619, when the first twenty black slaves were shipped to Jamestown, Virginia, to 1826, when John Russwurm graduated at Bowdoin College in Brunswick, Massachusetts, was a period of 207 years.

John Russwurm did not remain long in the United States. He, along with Samuel Cornish, established a newspaper called *Freedom's Journal*, in 1827, in New York. He worked hard for the freedom of black Americans, but he had little success in achieving his goal and concluded that black Americans would never be granted full citizenship in the United States. In frustration, Russwurm moved to Liberia, Africa, in 1829, where he died in 1851 at the age of 51.

What of the educational standing of black Americans in modern time?

CURRENT BLACK AMERICANS' EDUCATIONAL STATUS

Describing the inadequacies of black American education in modern time, the *New Catholic Encyclopedia* (Vol.10, 1967), says: "Although educational opportunities for Negroes have expanded considerably since the late 1930s, serious deficiencies remain. In the South, where the greatest inequities exist, as late as 1950, one in five Negro adults had completed no more than five years of formal schooling, only two in five had any high school education, and nearly three times as many Negroes as whites were functional illiterates. In the North, twice as many Negro adults as white adults had no high school education."

It was also a tug of war to admit some blacks into higher institutions of learning. Many of us still remember the celebrated case of James Meredith who was the first Negro to attend the University of Mississippi. Although he was accompanied by federal marshals so that he could register in the University for the fall of 1962, police and state officials repeatedly barred him from entering the campus. The riot that followed after Meredith finally succeeded in registering left two dead. Yet Meredith was born in Kosciusko, Mississippi! It is not too difficult to imagine how a person studying in such a hostile atmosphere will fare, yet thousands have attempted to do so.

Even today racial discrimination polarizes many college campuses. One such is Michigan State University at Ann Arbor where a student is reported to have said in a radio broadcast, "Do you know why black people smell? They smell so that white people will hate them."

Although efforts and appeals are being made to educate blacks, the Americans who were nearly not Americans still have a long way to go. Appeals, such as telethons, made for the United Negro College Fund help only to a small degree. Several decades may be needed to fill the gap of inaction and deprivation of educational opportunities.

This is especially demonstrated by the percentage of blacks who belong to professional groups in the United States. Blacks comprise about ten percent of the United States population, yet they make up *less than two percent of the professional population* such as doctors, dentists and lawyers. And blacks make up *less than one percent of the engineering population* in the U.S.

Professional sports is a field that once locked out black Americans. Black Americans were not signed up as professional sports players until after the Second World War, when the Los Angeles Dodgers signed the first black baseball player, Jackie Robinson, in 1947, reasoning that if blacks had laid their lives down side by side with whites in the world war, they should be able to participate equally in sports. Still, it was not until the fifties and the sixties that the acceptance of blacks into professional sporting arenas gained momentum. Today blacks abound in many professional sports, but some white owners are reluctant to pay black athletes the same salary as they pay their white colleagues or appoint them to managerial posts.

About baseball and blacks, for example, *Ebony* observed: "It's unbelievable that in the 35 years since Jackie Robinson broke the color barrier, and after all the Blacks that have come and gone, there are no Black managers in the game." [22] So while the lots of some blacks may have improved economically, the fact is that "the fight for freedom isn't over yet."

HOME UPBRINGING AND RACIAL PREJUDICE

Today, as in the past, there are many noble whites (Americans and non-Americans) who do not believe that blacks (or other colors) are inferior to whites. So, such civil persons accord all peoples, regardless of color, proper respect and treatment. But what is the root of racial discrimination? Racial discrimination usually stems from home training. Children, although almost insatiably curious, are not born racist.

Awake! magazine related this story:

One day a white schoolboy came home and said to his mother: "I have made a new friend at school. May I bring him home to play?"

"What color is he?" the mother inquired.

"I can't remember. Tomorrow I'll look and see." [23]

It seems crystal clear, then, that it is only when children grow up that they become discriminatory against people of other colors or languages. What has happened? Home training by racist parents or other adults is usually responsible. If children were not indoctrinated with racism, they would most likely grow up without being bigoted about people of other colors, languages or cultures. There is no doubt, then, that children should be given proper training, especially about how to regard fellow humans of other extractions.

You may contend that you know of many blacks who were raised in good environments, well-nourished, especially during the crucial, tender years of life, given the same opportunities as whites, and yet who do not measure up to their white colleagues, either at work or school. Why do such situations exist? First of all, many blacks who were given the same opportunities as whites usually measure up to whites. (It must be said, though, that there is a great variation in how people, whether of the same color or not, perform in a given task. The reasons for the vagaries in performance include: talent, interest, teaching method, time spent on studying, and disciplined home and school environment.) Regarding blacks who may fail to measure up with their colleagues, we like to point out that even if one was well-fed, raised in a good environment, given the same opportunities for advancement as whites, but not socially accepted, that can be detrimental to body and brain functions—as we will, among other things, discuss next.

NOTES

1. Dr. Manning Marable, "Beyond the Race—Class Dilemma," *The Nation*, April 11, 1981, Vol. 232, No. 14, p. 432.

2. Ibid., p. 432.

3. *Encyclopedia of Black America*, (New York, McGraw-Hill, 1981), p. 8.

4. Immigrants intended to serve in a colony, or persons under binding contract to work for others for an established period of time.

5. *The New Catholic Encyclopedia*, Vol. 3, 1967, p. 907.

6. Ibid., pp. 906-07.

7. "Searching For the Reason Why," *Time*, 27 July, 1981, p. 33.

8. Ibid., p. 33.

9. "Anger in the Streets," *Time*, July 20, 1981, p. 31.

10. Ibid., p. 32.

11. "Taking Stock of the Damage," *Newsweek*, 27 July, 1981, p. 35.

12. Vernon E. Jordan, "The Grim Outlook For Black Progress," *USA Today*, Nov., 1981, Vol. 110/2438, No. 81, p. 44.

13. Robert Pear, "Inflation Wiped Out Gains in Earnings in 70's," *New York Times*, 25 April, 1982, p. 1.

14. Kenneth B. Clark and Carl Gershman, "The Black Plight, Race or Class?" *New York Times Magazine*, 5 Oct. 1980, p. 4.

15. Vernon E. Jordan, *USA Today*, Nov., 1981, p. 44.

16. "Beyond the Race Class," *The Nation*, 11 April, 1981, p. 431.

17. *Statistical Abstract of the United States*, U.S. Department of Commerce, Bureau of Census, 1978.

18. Robert S. Goodhart and Maurice E. Shills, *Modern Nutrition in Health and Disease*, (Philadelphia, Lea & Febiger, 1980), pp. 700, 706.

19. *Man's Most Dangerous Myth*, p. 403.

20. Ibid., p. 388.

21. Kenneth B. Clark, "The Role of Race," *New York Times Magazine*, 5 Oct., 1980, p. 7.

22. Norman O. Unger, "Baseball 1980: 35 Years After Jackie Robinson," *Ebony*, June 1980, p. 105.

23. "The Races—What is Their Origin?" *Awake!*, 8 Feb. 1982, p. 12.

TEN

PSYCHOPHYSIOLOGY, ETHNOPSYCHOLOGY, ETHNOCENTRISM AND BLACKS

"I wish he had beaten me up and gotten it over with instead of him putting me down mentally. It's so difficult to endure mental abuse," a woman said about her husband.

Not only is prolonged mental torment difficult to endure, it can also trigger physical sickness. The interaction of the mind and the body is called psychophysiology, and people who are discriminated against by the society can suffer from adverse psychophysiological factors.

PSYCHOPHYSIOLOGY AND HOSTILE SOCIAL ARENA

The *World Book Dictionary* (Vol. 2, 1983), defines psychophysiology as "the branch of physiology which deals with mental phenomena." And the effects the mind has upon the body is often referred to as psychosomatic: "having to do with, or caused by the interaction of mind and body, especially in development of bodily disorders related to mental or emotional disturbances." What do respected authorities say cause adverse psychophysiological (or psychosomatic) reactions? And can what they say be applied to discrimination in the human social arena?

Renowned doctors and nutritionists all agree that stress can drain the body of vital proteins, minerals and vitamins. Dr. Arthur Furst, a toxicologist and cancer researcher at the University of San Francisco, California, has said that, while the body is equipped to handle normal stress, "unusual stresses" will deplete the body of vitamin C and thereby affect adversely the body's self-immunization. Also, sustained stress can deplete the body's store of zinc. Zinc plays a definite and important part in "skin tone, wound healing and general well-being."

Highlighting the interaction of the mind with physical health, Dr. Caroline B. Thomas, professor emeritus at the Johns Hopkins University School of Medicine and head of the Precursors Study, says:

> "What is stamina?" Dr. Thomas defines it partly the way the dictionary does: the strength to withstand disease, fatigue or hardship. But she also incorporates a quality of resilience and stability. *Stamina is a harmony between mind and body that is a product of our genes, our attitudes and our upbringing.*
>
> What creates stamina? The important elements are an open, flexible approach to life; self-esteem; a spontaneous, outgoing temperament; and *a minimum of tension, depression, anxiety and anger while under stress."* As Dr. Thomas says, "Stamina is what separates winners and losers in life. It determines whether you go through life with your nose a half-inch above water or a half-inch below." [1] (Italics ours.)

Obviously social unrest can trigger an unhealthy interaction between the body and the mind, but can a hostile environment affect brain structure?

PSYCHOPHYSIOLOGY, BRAIN STRUCTURE AND SOCIAL UNREST

Throwing further light on how the mind interacts with the body, Harvard biologist Richard Lewontin says it is "a complicated feedback loop between thought and action." It has been discovered, according to *Reader's Digest* of September, 1981, that social setbacks and the like can affect the hormones produced by the body. The article, entitled "Male/Female: The *Other* Difference," cites the example of how social setbacks affected rhesus monkeys. It says: "Studies show that testosterone levels drop in male rhesus monkeys after they suffer a social setback and surge up when they experience a triumph. Other experiments indicate that emotional stress can change hormonal patterns in pregnant female rodents, which in turn may *affect the structure of the fetal brain.* By processes still not understood, biology seems susceptible to social stimuli." [2] (Italics ours.)

The same effects of social relapse on monkeys may be applicable to humans. There is hardly any doubt that bad news, stress, blows to the ego, and a generally unhappy situation adversely affect sexual function in humans. Sexual drive may decline greatly. In fact, stressful situations can contribute to the inability of a man to father a child, or of a woman to become pregnant. The male sperm cells, for example, may experience aberration, such as being formed with two heads instead of one. The female, on the other hand, may be unable to produce mature egg cells in the ovaries, which are then released to the womb to join the male's sperm cell. (And where pregnancy occurs, the baby may not be as physically and mentally healthy as it should be.) In some cases, extreme stress has resulted in temporary impotency for the male. When, however, conditions become normal, their sexual function is usually restored. Happy couples make better lovers.

The point of intense interest, however, is that social setback or rejection, as experienced by black Americans, can have adverse physiological effects. Many diseases or illnesses can be caused by psychophysiological reasons.

You may recall, as discussed in chapter three, that the pituitary gland plays a vital role not only in skin pigmentation, but also in the production of adrenaline, thyroid function, and sexual function. Therefore, when a person is met with great disappointment, social setback and so forth, the pituitary gland is usually stimulated to produce adrenaline. While the presence or feeling of adrenaline in your system may warn you of danger and prepare you to take certain action, excessive and prolonged production of adrenaline is detrimental to the body. It becomes a stressing, rather than benevolent, situation. Adrenaline induced by negative emotions can, if prolonged, cause a number of adverse effects in the body. These include increased blood pressure, increased heartbeat, and the constriction of arteries leading to the heart. Inordinate release of adrenaline can also cause hypoglycemia, or an unhealthy increase in blood sugar.

So the Bible is quite correct when it says: "Being cheerful keeps you healthy. It is slow death to be gloomy all the time" (Proverbs 17:27; Good News Bible). On the other hand, "Kind words are like honey—sweet to the taste and good for your health" (Proverbs 16:24; GNB).

No doubt many black Americans suffer from psychophysiological ills brought upon by social rejection.

Our earlier quotation from the *Reader's Digest* says: ". . . emotional stress can change hormonal patterns in pregnant female rodents, which in turn may affect the structure of the fetal brain."

Can unfavorable social conditions also affect adversely the brain of a developing baby in the womb? Yes. Doctors say that babies are highly susceptible to their environment—both inside and outside the womb. Hence some infants[3] are born whining abnormally because their prenatal environmental was not favorable. If unfavorable circumstances can precipitate miscarriage or a whining baby, it is also possible that a baby's brain "structure" or function may have been impaired so subtly that it is not generally perceptible. This condition may become extremely critical if the child is then prohibited from being educated, is undernourished, and, to add insult to injury, socially rejected and judicially disadvantaged. Some British, American and South African blacks show the effects we have been describing.

PSYCHOPHYSIOLOGY AND FEMALE'S MENTAL STRUCTURE AND FUNCTION

There are, of course, a multitude of things that can affect mental function and retardation; these include nutrition, chemicals, drugs, smoking, and excessive intake of alcohol. However, evidence shows that females are, *by heredity*, not as susceptible to mental malfunction as are men. Why so?

First of all, most females are more comfortable with their emotions. They usually release built-up emotions through various means, such as talking or crying, whereas most men are reluctant to shed tears, thinking that it is not masculine or is too demeaning. Moreover, most men have the habit of bottling-up their emotions by not talking about their problems.[4] Or as Dr. Joyce Brothers puts it in *What Every Woman Should Know About Men:* "[Men] talk about themselves less, but they worry about themselves more." In any event, these problems, if prolonged and intensified, may heavily task both body and mind. Such suppressed emotions may lead to mental disorder—if only temporarily.

Let us listen to a psychiatrist: "Says psychiatrist Smoller, 'People who don't deal well with emotions often get a physical disease instead.' People who can't easily express their feelings frequently submerge them, and this, he says, can upset the 'fine interaction' between body and mind. When the stress is big enough, and the ability to tolerate it is small, illness can result."[5]

Because men frequently submerge their emotions, and women often let theirs flow free, women seem to have generally better mental health than men. Also, the organization of the brains of the sexes is different.

The article quoted earlier, "Male/Female: The *Other* Difference" has this to say:

For years researchers have known that men's and women's mental functions are organized somewhat differently. Men appear to have more "laterality"—that is, their functions are separately controlled by the left or right hemisphere of the brain, while women's seem *diffused* through both hemispheres. The first clue to this intriguing disparity came from victims of brain damage. Doctors noticed that male patients were much likelier to suffer speech impairment after damage to the left hemisphere and loss of such non-verbal functions as visual-spatial ability when the right hemisphere was damaged. *Women showed less* functional loss, regardless of the hemisphere involved. Some researchers believe this is because women's brain activity is duplicated in both hemispheres. Women usually mature earlier than men, which means that their hemispheric processes may have less time to draw apart. They retain more nerve-transmission mechanisms in the connective tissue between the two hemispheres and may thus be better able to coordinate the efforts of both hemispheres. (Italics ours.)

Let us employ statistics to further establish our point that the female brain seems more resilient than the male's.

According to *Statistical Abstract of the United States*, 1980, a total of 434,000 people were being cared for at "mental hospitals and residential treatment centers" in 1970. Of this figure, 245,000 were males and 189,000 were females. This figure is not just a reflection of a peculiar time period. For example, a total of 630,000 persons were in mental institutions in the United States in 1960. Out of that number, 336,000 were males whereas 294,000 were females. It should be noted that more males were in mental institutions than females not because there were more males in the United States, especially in 1970, than there were females. The opposite was true: more females than males. The United States' population of males in 1970 was 97,469,000 whereas the female population was 102,860,000. Yet more males were in mental institutions than females.

Current discoveries, tests and experiments, indicate this to be true: that there are both functional and structural differences in the brains of males and females. Also, there is no doubt that men and women respond differently to the same situation. Men may be more logical in their approach to a problem, especially of an emotional or family nature, whereas women tend to yield to emotions. Since men and women in general do not respond the same way in a given situation, it logically follows that their brains must have been structured differently.

Let us now apply the resiliency in the female's brain to the part it has been playing in the role of black American women in the family arena.

BLACK AMERICAN WOMEN IN THE FAMILY ARENA

The fact that women's minds seem to be more resilient than men's in emotionally-tasking situations may be why black American women are able to stand behind their families while many black American males may walk out on their families, due, perhaps, to the onslaught of social pressures. So many successful black American males and females attribute their success to their mothers, sometimes saying, "I did it for my mother." Whereas white American males usually play a major role in the success of their offspring. The self-confidence of white male is intact. He can walk tall where others are crouching. The feeling of self-confidence is helpful in raising a family.

It must be admitted that there are men in all color groups who are not capable of shouldering responsibility in their households as they should. However, the incidence of family abandonment is higher among black American males than any other color group in the United States. Moreover, we must not forget that Africans do not have the traits of abandoning their families or evading vital family matters on which decisions have to be made. Yet blacks were brought to the Americas from Africa. Furthermore, blacks living in the Caribbean where they are the dominant color group, or where they are not subjected to social rejection on racial grounds, do not seem to have the peculiar traits of walking away from their families or shirking family responsibilities as black American males do. It appears, therefore, that the feeling of inadequacy in the family was later developed by male black Americans due to pressures brought upon them by racial upheavals and rejection.

Does social pressure also contribute to the high rate of divorce among black American families?

BLACK AMERICANS AND HIGH RATE OF DIVORCE

While divorce, separation, and desertion occur everywhere, the degree to which black Americans suffer from those social ills is unique. *Encyclopedia Americana* (Vol. 9, 1979) says: "Divorce and separation rates of blacks in the United States are much higher than those of whites. It was formerly thought that this difference in rates was attributable to the low socio-economic status of blacks. But analysis of census data has shown that when blacks and whites of the same educational, occupational, or income level are compared, marital instability for blacks is one and a half to two times as great as for whites. Adequate explanations for the racial difference in divorce rates are not available."

Also citing an inordinately high rate of divorce among black Americans is the *New York Times* of May 24, 1982, which says that blacks' divorces are "more than double whites' and Hispanics." For every 1,000 black marriages, 203 ended in divorce, compared to a rate of only ninety-two for whites and ninety-four for Hispanics.

The following statistics from the same publication prove our point a little more forcefully.

FOR EVERY 1,000 MARRIAGES   [7]

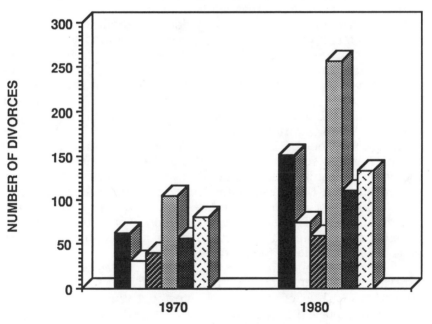

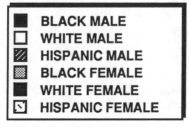

- ■ BLACK MALE
- □ WHITE MALE
- ▨ HISPANIC MALE
- ▧ BLACK FEMALE
- ■ WHITE FEMALE
- ◩ HISPANIC FEMALE

Dr. Stuart A. Taylor, an industrial psychologist in New York and Washington, D.C., shows that disparities in education of the black man and woman can precipitate divorce. For example, intellectual incompatibility can hinder communication—the lifeblood of any relationship, but especially marriage. This, in turn, can result in emotional and physical incompatibility. Supporting further his opinion, Doctor Taylor said: "The divorce rate for black women increases as her educational and professional level increases, whereas that is not so for white women. The divorce rate is about ten percent higher for black women who are college graduates and that divorce rate increases to fifteen percent for black women with college degrees and one year of graduate school and to nineteen percent for two years or more of graduate school." [6]

It should be borne in mind that there are white, Hispanic and Oriental women who are married to men whose educational levels are below theirs, yet that inequality does not seem to have resulted in a high rate of divorce among those color groups. The same is also true of women and men in the rest of the world, especially in Africa where many men are half-educated or completely uneducated. A woman could be happily married to a man with less education if he has self-confidence and is willing and able to shoulder family responsibilities. On the other hand, if a couple is well-educated but the male is lacking in the above-stated qualities, the marriage may not be a happy one. Admittedly, sound education could engender self-confidence, but one does not have to have so many letters behind one's name to have faith in oneself. You may also recall that the *Encyclopedia Americana* we referred to said: "But analysis of census data has shown that when blacks and whites of *the same educational, occupational, or income are compared,* marital instability for blacks is one and a half to two times as great as for whites." (Italics ours.)

It seems obvious, therefore, that the marriages of many black Americans end up in divorce, not so much due to inequality in education which is, of course, a seeming contributory factor, but to psychophysiological misfortunes they have suffered. Doctor Taylor himself seems to touch on this when he said: "The [black] man has tended to miss out on a lot of things and what he's been through is not that great, so *he reinforces his disappointment on the black woman.*" [8] (Italics ours.)

Dr. Alvin F. Poussaint, an associate professor of psychiatry at Harvard Medical School, agreed that the high rate of divorce among black Americans stems from social rejection which, inevitably, is psychologically and psychophysiologically devastating. He states: "Blacks face more economic circumstances because of discrimination and lack of seniority in the work force. These circumstances stoke frustrations by making it more difficult to succeed, and they sometimes lead to a *sense of powerlessness.*

"*Social conditions* facing blacks, including subtle and blatant racism, make black marriages more fragile." [9] (Italics ours.)

Commenting further on family breakdown among black Americans, the *New York Times* of May 24, 1982 made this observation: "An array of complex, stressful factors that are a special part of black experience in America has blended with the normal pressures of marriage to produce a soaring divorce rate among blacks, according to experts on the black family."

Finally, Dr. Price M. Cobbs, a San Francisco psychiatrist, definitely agreed that the root of the breakdown in black American marriages was psychological. He said: "They are still working out whether they can be black and middle-class at the same time, which impacts on people's ability to get along. In the 1960s blacks began to define themselves narrowly and, to be black, you had to be poverty-stricken, and if you had a job or were successful, you weren't black. And to the extent there are still a lot of these unanswered questions, that impacts on the divorce rate." [10]

And the impact on the divorce rate is shown by the alarmingly progressive increase in the number of households headed by black American women.

FEMALE FAMILY HOUSEHOLDS

According to 1980 *Statistical Abstract of the United States,* there were 77,330,000 households in the United States in 1979. Whites' households in that year were 50, 910,000, and blacks households 5,918,000. What percentage of the numbers of households between these two color-groups was without the presence of a man? The table below and other statistics that follow show:

FEMALE FAMILY HOUSEHOLDERS [11] BY RACE AND PRESENCE OF CHILDREN *(Statistics are for 1979)*					
COLOR-GROUPS	YEAR AND PERCENTAGE OF TOTAL HOUSEHOLDS				
	1960	1965	1970	1975	1979
White	8.1	9.0	9.0	10.5	11.6
Black [12]	20.9	23.7	28.3	35.3	40.5

It is obvious from this table that "female family householders" of blacks in the United States are disproportionately and alarmingly higher than those of whites.

"Households and Families by Type of Householder" *(No Children Involved)*

White Females

White Female Householder - "no spouse present" - but old enough to marry, or have married without children, separated, divorced, deserted: 5,918,000 (1979). Percentage of all white families: 11.6.

Black Females

Black Female Householder - "no spouse present" - but old enough to marry, or have married without children, separated, divorced deserted: 2,540,000 (1979). That figure is 36.8 percent of all black households in the United States in 1979.

Evidently, racial pressures from society seem responsible for continuing family disintegration among black Americans. A person who feels frustrated by the society is like a person who feels frustrated with his job. Upon whom is he likely to explode his pent-up emotions? Those who are closest to him—members of his family.

Social turmoil may also have triggered a disease whose inordinate occurrence among black Americans is a mystery.

"THE SILENT KILLER" AND BLACK AMERICANS

It is a well-known fact that black Americans, as a distinct color group, suffer from inordinate incidents of hypertension. Regarding this lethal disease, William M. Manger, M.D., Ph.D., chairman of the National Hypertension Association, have this to say: "In the U.S., essential hypertension occurs more frequently, more severely, and earlier in blacks than in whites, 30 percent of adult blacks and 15 to 20 percent of white adults develop it; men get it more than women. Recent studies have shown that high blood pressure affects a significant number of children at a very young age—and higher percentage of black [children] than white children." [13] Echoing the same opinion is *Science* of June 1979. It says: "It is well known that the mortality and prevalence of hypertension in the Untied States are higher in black persons than in whites."

One can suffer from hypertension for various reasons, such as deficient diet, too much intake of salt, obesity, sustained stress, insecurity, anxiety, constant eruption of violent anger or sustained hostility. All these things do, of course, affect people in every part of the world. However, the societies in Britain, South Africa and the United States undoubtedly aggravate those destructive elements in blacks. It is not impossible, therefore, that the continued social unrest is responsible for the high risk of hypertension among black Americans. Doctors themselves admit that "not all cases of hypertension are alike. The causes can vary, and, in 90 percent of patients, they are unknown" (*Harper's Bazaar*, October, 1978).

Doctors also say that tension can cause high blood pressure. Your own personal experience of life may have confirmed that. However, respected professional findings are appropriate here.

Readers' Digest of March 1983 made this observation, using the documented report of a man called Jim:

Jim's case illustrates the powerful role that attitude plays in physical health. It also shows the impact childhood experiences exert on adult health. Although most cases are less direct than Jim's, there *is* strong evidence that childhood events—in addition to genes—may well trigger such midlife maladies as cancer, heart disease and mental illness.

To understand these links and triggers is to be better able to identify them and minimize their effects on ourselves and on our children. Dr. Brian Schulman, an assistant clinical professor of psychiatry of Georgetown University School of Medicine in Washington, D.C., says 'To look for a single factor for disease is wrong. We have to be looking for a bio-psychosocial model.' This would include the condition of our body, *our psychological state and our social adjustment* as a way of determining our potential for illness. [14] (Italics ours.)

The most tragic aspect of this is that the above adverse condition can begin, and often does, in childhood. The same publication continues:

Those most vulnerable to life's stresses—and premature disease—may be continually compromised by the chronic, often subconscious stresses and emotions that originated in childhood. It is now believed that passive emotional states such as grief and *hopelessness* trigger responses in the brain. Long-term, unconscious stresses in particular can cause chronic secretion of cortisol, which may undermine the immune system and its resistance to arthritis, cancer and infectious diseases.

Aggressive emotions such as anger and impatience apparently release hormones and chemicals known as catecholamines, of which adrenaline is one. The release of adrenaline, which greatly increases strength, can be vital for survival; but prolonged or frequent release can bring on *high blood pressure*, which can lead to headaches, heart attack, stroke or kidney problems.

The body is always seeking homeostasis, its own equilibrium. Under stress, it attempts to compensate by activating biochemical changes, and the price we pay for that can be a greater vulnerability to disease. The disease we get—if any—may be determined by our own particular genetic vulnerability. (Italics ours.)

The association of social oppression, mysteriously high rate of hypertension deaths and other sicknesses among black Americans is, therefore, not unfounded.

Ethnopsychology is another factor that affects minority groups, especially blacks, in the United States.

ETHNOPSYCHOLOGICAL FACTOR AMONG BLACK AMERICANS

A dictionary simply defines ethnopsychology as "the psychology of races and peoples." But the definition of psychology in the same dictionary aids us greatly to appreciate the impact of ethnopsychology. Psychology—a common word to most people—is defined as: "Science of mind or mental phenomena and activities; the science of behavior; the study of the interactions between the biological organism (as man) and its physical and social environment. The *mental, attitudinal, motivational, or behavioral* characteristics of an individual or a type, class, or group of individuals." (Italics ours.)

So ethnopsychological factors can affect the mental attitude and behavior of a color group that is at disadvantage. The physical health of such a color group can also be favorably or unfavorably affected. The effects of physiopsychology are similar to that of ethnopsychology. The difference between physiopsychology and ethnopsychology is that the effects of the former can be felt by all people, whereas the action of the latter is directed to a color or ethnic group.

Well, do blacks living in the United States, Britain and South Africa suffer from ethnopsychological factors, or believe that they are inferior to whites?

That the black man may be suffering from an inferiority complex has been commented upon and documented. For example, Audrey B. Chapman, family therapist at Howard University Counseling Service in Washington, D.C. commented: "The black man has been stripped of having any economic power, and, therefore, has been constantly dealing with feeling impotent in the global sense, in the community and in the family. That has got to have an impact on his *self-esteem* and the way he feels free to operate in the context of the family." [15] (Italics ours.)

James Farmer, writing in *Today's Education*, used his father as a classic case to show that an inferiority complex may not be farfetched among black Americans:

> People's images of themselves do not change easily, however. My father, for example, was a Biblical scholar. He was a Ph.D. in Old Testament and Hebrew from Boston University, the first black with a Ph.D. in the state of Texas. He could speak, read, write, and think in many languages, including Hebrew, Greek, Aramaic, Latin, French, German, Spanish. Despite all his accomplishments, in his heart of hearts my father believed that whites were superior, blacks were inferior. He had been conditioned by everything he had read growing up as a child in South Carolina and Georgia and by all of the instruments for dissemination of culture that determined what he thought.[16]

Further reasons why black Americans and blacks in Britain may suffer from inferiority complex include the fact that they grow up in a society where the color of skin is predominantly white. Manufactured goods, scientific and technological ingenuities around them, their rulers, business tycoons, bankers, employers, supervisors, and so forth, are almost all white. Blacks in other countries are not advanced scientifically or technologically either. In such a situation, it is natural to feel inferior, even if one is as competent, or more competent, than the other person. On the other hand, not to feel inferior is unnatural. In fact, if one shows a complete feeling of well-being, both physically and mentally, in situation of such great disparity, it may mean that one has no actively discerning mind.

SUPERIORITY COMPLEX

While a black person may suffer from inferiority complex, a white person may feel superiority complex because of the reasons mentioned in the previous paragraph. Where others stoop, the white man can walk tall because of his skin color. In fact, it has been said that you can hardly be luckier than to be a white male in American society, and that is certainly true of other societies, especially Britain and South Africa.

However, it should be noted that only a handful of whites (or other colors) are inventors or scientific geniuses. Such few inventors and outstanding scientists have a positive and abiding social influence on the entire communities of whites, even though millions of whites are extremely limited in scientific knowledge and are not inventors, yet they may put on an air of superiority just because they happen to be of the same color of skin of great scientists or the inventors.

Does this mean that no whites suffer from inferiority complex? No. Inferiority and superiority complexes come in all colors, even the most ignorant may put on an air of superiority complex. No matter who we are, we all feel inadequate one time or another. But when it comes to dealing with other skin colors on social levels, many mask their insecurity and inferiority complex by engaging in blatant discrimination and violent actions. They claim, without supportive evidence, that the "black race" or the "white race" is superior. If you delve deeply into the lives of some of the leaders of such groups, you may find that they are cowards and very unsure of themselves, and that they practice racial discrimination to feel accepted by the skin color of the group they belong. *The Race Question in Modern Science* put it quite appropriately:

> It would appear that those *most insistent* on discrimination against Negroes [or against whites] are the lower class whites [or blacks]; they are the first to fear Negro competition in the economic field, and as they have no other argument to warrant their attitude of superiority toward Negroes, they rely on skin pigmentation to which they give an altogether exaggerated importance.[17]

BLACKS IN AFRICA AND THE CARIBBEAN

But what about blacks in Africa and other parts of the world? Do they suffer from an inferiority complex? No, because they grew up in environments where the color of their skin is not a social issue. However, blacks wonder why whites have a lion's share of scientific and technological advancement. Hence they respect whites, especially where there is no nationalistic or political turmoil. Nonetheless, blacks in the U.S., Britain and South Africa are at a disadvantage ethnopsychologically.

One of the unwanted and bloodthirsty babies of ethnopsychology is ethnocentrism.

ETHNOCENTRISM

The *World Book Encyclopedia* (Vol. 6, 1977) describes ethnocentrism as "a universal belief in the superiority of one's culture, and a parallel hostility and suspicion toward other cultures." "Belief in the superiority of one's culture" can, for example, make a white person think that other color groups are not as developed scientifically and technologically as whites because whites have a superior culture. On the other hand, an Oriental may think that the eastern culture excels over the western culture, because crimes and violence are more prevalent in the West than in the East. One thing is common with both kinds of persons: they are ethnocentric.

Basically the practice of ethnocentrism is the practice of selfishness, of self-centeredness. *Encyclopedia Americana* (Vol. 10, 1979) says: Ethnocentrism "is the tendency of human groups to judge external phenomena with reference to attitudes and values that are specific to the group" and the "wariness and distrust of outside groups and a belief in the unquestioned superiority of one's own people."

For these reasons, a color- or ethnic-group may promote only the interest of its own group and remain indifferent to the needs of others. That is why there are different ethnic group organizations all over the world.

That is also why there are bloody clashes all over the world among ethnic groups, especially in South Africa, Britain and the United States. One color group may fight another over such issues as employment opportunities, educational facilities, and the freedom to live in the area one desires. Legal battles about employment in the United States have resulted in what is called "reverse discrimination."

The comment made by *The Nation* of April 11, 1981, therefore seems appropriate: "Racism, then, is not merely intolerance toward blacks, or the 'superstructural justification of the exploitation of black labor, or the collective projection of white psychosexual neuroses.' It is all of these elements and more; its roots in Western capitalism society and culture are deep and pervasive." [18]

Because blacks living in the United States and Britain are not fully accepted by whites, and yet the blacks have nowhere else to go, they suffer from identity crisis. The condition of black South Africans is, as we all know, worse.

Nonetheless, do people really hate or discriminate because of color of skin?

NOTES

1. John Pekkanen, "Keys to a Longer, Healthier Life," *Reader's Digest*, Vol. 122, No. 731, March, 1983, p. 28.

2. "Male/Female: The *Other* Difference," *Reader's Digest*, Vol. 119, No. 713, September, 1981, p. 132.

3. Some children seem to be immune to unfavorable atmosphere both inside and outside the womb. Such children that triumph over general adverse conditions with impunity are, however, exceptions rather than the rule.

4. This may be one of the reasons why women almost everywhere in the world live longer than men.

5. John Pekkanen, "Keys to a Longer, Healthier Life," *Reader's Digest*, Vol. 122, No. 731, March, 1983, p. 28.

6. Stuart A. Taylor, *New York Times*, May 24, 1982, p. 16.

7. Sheila Rule, "Black Divorces Soar; Experts Cite Special Strains," *New York Times*, 24 May, 1982, p. 16.

8. Ibid., p. 16.

9. Dr. Alvin F. Poussaint, *New York Times*, May 24, 1982, p. 16.

10. Dr. Price M. Cobbs, *New York Times*, May 24, 1982, p. 16.

11. Statistical Abstract of the United States, publisher, 1980.

12. Figures include other ethnic groups, such as Mexican Americans, and Orientals. However, divorce, separation and desertion rates are negligible among these color groups, but especially the Orientals.

13. Dr. William M. Manger and Dr. Irvine H. Page, "Hypertension, the Silent Killer," *Harper's Bazaar*, No. 3203, Oct. 1978, p. 94.

14. John Pekkanen, "Keys to a Longer, Healthier Life," *Reader's Digest*, Vol. 122, No. 731, March 1983, pp. 26, 30.

15. "Black Divorces Soar; Experts Cite Special Strains," *New York Times*, May 24, 1982, p. 16.

16. James Farmer, "Human Rights: A National Perspective, 'If Not Now, When?'", *Today's Education*, Vol. 702, April/May, 1981, p. 15.

17. UNESCO, *The Race Question in Modern Science*, p. 27.

18. Dr. Manning Marable, "Beyond The Race—Class Dilemma," *The Nation*, 11 April 1981, p. 432.

ELEVEN

DO PEOPLE REALLY HATE
THE COLOR OF SKIN?

Racial discrimination is everywhere, yet many of us may be unconscious of the fact that discrimination is not primarily motivated by color of skin. *If color of skin were the dominant reason why people discriminate, it would be virtually impossible for people of different colors of skin to ever love and respect one another,* for the color would always be a barrier. What, then, is the chief reason people discriminate against people of a different color?

Because of what the color represents, or the images it sends to the mind, which are largely determined by a person's knowledge and experience of that color group. Nonetheless, a person's knowledge and experience of a color group do not epitomize, to any great degree of accuracy, the virtues and vices of all the individuals who belong to that color group.

Let us illustrate our point. In the western world, discrimination against a white person on the basis of color does not exist—even in imagination. But that is not necessarily true in other parts of the world, say the Orient. When China temporarily opened its door to the western world, foreigners had a fair degree of freedom to mix with Chinese. That freedom does not exist anymore. The government discouraged it on the basis that socializing with foreigners could be dangerous to the Chinese people's health. Put bluntly, that the Chinese could contract foreign maladies. Most likely many Chinese believed what their government said about socializing with foreigners. And most of the foreigners who have been flocking to China are whites from Europe and the United States.

Whenever the Chinese who believe what their government

says about foreigners see white people, what kind of image is that color likely to produce in their minds? That here are people from whom they might contract diseases—real or imagined. The Chinese, like other people, will also associate white skin with technological advancement.

Similarly, most South African blacks and many black Americans will look at white skin as a symbol of cruelty and oppression. Hence, it is not uncommon for a black American to say, "I don't trust white people." Conversely, a white person may say, "I don't like black people." But in each case it is not the color that is at issue, but the images it sends to the mind.

Personal relationships can also be used to prove this point about the color of skin. No doubt all of us have been physically attracted to someone who becomes repelling after we really know him or her closely. On the other hand, we may have grown to love a person whose exterior may not be exactly as ours, or be that appealing. What happened in both situations? Our mental image of the person has changed.

SPORTS, ENTERTAINMENT AND COLOR

In the entertainment world and in sports, feelings of discrimination usually evaporate. A black actor or actress, or a singer, is usually well liked by all. Very few people discriminate against a good athlete, regardless of his color. On the contrary, he is often given a great accolade and standing ovations. And we all know how fans react when a game gets really exciting—regardless of what color the players are. Whites acquire pictures and autographs of black entertainers and sports personalities. Blacks also acquire the pictures and autographs of white entertainers and sports personalities. Again, the people love the public personalities, not because of their color, but because of the images they send to the mind.

So if all of a sudden black nations become scientific and technological giants, positive images of blacks may be produced, yet the color has not changed, only the mental image associated with it. The Japanese demonstrate this point. They are now well advanced in the fields of science and technology, and so respect for them by white communities has soared. It was not always that way. So if black nations become technological giants, disregard for them will gradually disappear, and regard for them will steadily increase.

DIFFERENT COLORS AT PEACE—SAME COLOR FIGHTING

International situations can also be used to show that color is not the main reason people love or hate one another. Such situations include the war between Catholics and Protestants in Northern Ireland, the war between Christians and Muslims in Lebanon, between Iran and Iraq, and the divisions of North and South Korea. All these people are of the same color of skin. True, political, economic, religious, philosophical and other reasons are responsible for the enmity. The fact remains that, though of the same color, they hate each other. Yet these people may shower others of different colors with love, especially if those others approve their course.

Another international example of same-color enmity is the explosive situation between the Soviet Union and the United States. The two nations are implacable enemies. They gloat over each other's failure, and sorrow over each other's success, yet they are of the same color of skin. Whereas these two nations are friendly to other nations whose dominant skin color is not the same as theirs, but who share the ideologies of the superpowers.

Be that as it may, how do we explain the militant attitude among black Americans?

BLACK AMERICANS AND MILITANCY

We know that all humans have aggressive behavior. However, excessive aggressive attitudes were developed among black Americans because of the social inequalities and environmental impacts upon them. This kind of attitude is manifested in other areas of their lives, including that of the family, where problems may be handled belligerently. It is not easy for one to develop an amicable temperament if one has been reacting to a hostile environment all his life. Hostility and anger are as contagious as happiness and laughter.

This kind of militant attitude can develop wherever people are subjected to the same social conditions to which black Americans are subjected. The Asian Indians, for example, are very mild and extremely yielding. The South African Indians, however, whose ancestors originally emigrated from India, are extremely militant. They, too, are experiencing the discriminatory pressures of a racist society.

Another good example is Northern Ireland where constant and perennial terror reigns among Catholics and Protestants. Their children, conceived and raised in an environment rife with hostilities, have been galvanized into terrorism. What applies to

Northern Ireland applies to Lebanon to a greater degree of violence.

Perhaps the most important argument for black Americans' militancy being a cultivated trait is the fact that Africans are not as militant as black Americans. Yet, black Americans were taken as slaves from Africa to the Americas. Politics and tribal frictions do induce violent outbursts in Africa, as they do in other countries, but these are of a different nature from the militancy among blacks in the United States. However, in South Africa, where there are segregation and oppression, militancy also exists among blacks.

That blacks, either in the United States, Britain or South Africa, are not by nature more belligerent than other people seems supported by the comment made by the New Republic of July 3, 1965. It said that blacks in the United States are a "population capable of rioting, but not inevitably committed to it." We, of course, know why they riot: "execrable housing conditions, pervasive hopelessness." New York's Mayor Koch said, "The conditions of the urban centers are abominable."

We can understand, then, why Benjamin Hooks, executive director of the National Association for the Advancement of Colored People said: "I would pray and hope and work that there would be no more violence in our cities this summer [1980]. But when you have these kinds of depressed conditions, you create a classic symptom for a riot." [1]

Carl Gershman, former Fellow at the Non-Conservative Freedom House, seemed to sum up the reason behind black militancy by saying: "The sad irony in all of this is that what appears to be a form of racial militancy was, in reality, a policy of racial accommodation." [2]

Obviously, when social accommodation is achieved, either in the United States, Britain and especially in South Africa, belligerent actions of a racial nature will also vanish. But in the meantime, we do not want to forget that "social stimuli" do affect biological, attitudinal, behavioral and psychological functions.

SHOULD YOU LOVE YOURSELF?

To really love others you must love yourself first. No, we are not here talking about narcissism—abnormal self-love, self-admiration, or self-worship. Rather, we mean being pleased or satisfied with what you are as a human being.

To illustrate this, let me introduce an English acquaintance named Cornelius—an unusual name for an English man.

Cornelius was about fifty-five years old. He had a hoarse voice; he was slow-talking, cheerless, non-smiling, stern-looking, but had a firm and almost wrinkle-free face. Generally, Cornelius was unperturbably slow, and he would walk cautiously as if he were expecting some sort of an attack. He seemed always to wear the same clothes, and the clothes never looked clean nor dirty, nor ironed. Cornelius, in his khaki clothes, looked as if he had just been inducted into a half-disciplined army. I never knew Cornelius to have a kind word for anybody or show, either by what he said or did or by bodily reaction, that he was afraid of anybody. He would castigate everyone equally, either with words or by unintelligible or unsavory murmurings, tacit looks, or disapproving facial expressions. About the only time he seemed relaxed, contented and showed a miserly grin was when somebody met with a serious personal tragedy. So, good news of great joy would cast great gloom upon him. On the other hand, news of great calamity would make Cornelius happy almost to the point of celebration.

One afternoon, when there was no good news I knew of that would depress him so that he would not act as his normal self, I finally confronted him with the question: "Cornelius, do you like me?"

He snapped back an emphatic "No," as if he had been dying to let me know that he did not like me.

"Why is it, Cornelius, that you don't like me?"

"I don't even like myself," he shot back, "much less you." Grumbling, displaying his fist, gnashing his teeth, Cornelius left in a huff. But the point we are getting at is, since Cornelius did not like himself as he was, as a human, he could not be expected to like others. And he did not. Hence, he went about his daily affairs with a "chip on his shoulder" and dwelt in a pessimistic world where he expected the worst for others, and, perhaps, for himself, too.

This incident underscores why people may not express love to others. And because of the oppression and social upheavals with which blacks in South Africa, Britain and the United States have been afflicted, there may be a tendency for them to be gloomy about themselves. Certainly, they do not like their status as a color group.

How this kind of social hatred devastates people is shown by the way I once heard a black American refer to himself: "I'm a big black ugly Nigger." Unfortunately he was not joking. He kept putting himself down by what he said and did. He also attempted suicide several times. He may still be alive today or he may have taken his own life. The fact remains, however, that he belittled himself because he was utterly displeased with his life.

While you may not be able to make a person love himself, individuals or the society can precipitate a person to lose self-worth, yes, hate himself.

To stave off feelings of self-devaluation or inferiority, unwarranted militancy may be displayed by some blacks in a situation where you would not expect such militancy. To overcome feelings of inferiority, the slogan "Black is Beautiful" was adopted by black Americans, and the black power sign invented. Also, a black person may display an inappropriately hostile attitude to a white person, as a reaction to feeling that whites do not like him. Memories of past oppression and present social inequalities may stir up hatred in the minds of many blacks against whites. The black person also displays a hostile attitude towards fellow blacks. As color prejudice decreases, deep trust for others will commensurably increase. This will be to the happiness of all.

Loud talking is another thing black Americans are said to be guilty of.

BLACKS, POOR PEOPLE AND NOISE

Needless to say, every color of the human race has both its vices and virtues. Some are inherited, others are cultivated. It has been noticed that black Americans make more noise than whites. Is it because blacks are by nature different from whites, or Orientals, who are reputed to be almost saintly quiet?

Of course, not all blacks are noisy, and not all whites and Orientals are quiet. People who are poor and less educated, regardless of color, are usually noisier than the rest of the society. Since the majority of blacks fall into that category, we can understand why they may appear to be noisier than other color groups. Blacks who live in integrated neighborhoods are more quiet, though there may be some exceptions, white or black. Also, because poor people, often with large families, cram into small living quarters is all the more reason for them to be abnormally noisy. It also seems that poor people are noisy, either through music or vocal cord, in order to combat frustration or establish self-identity.

AFRICANS, NOISE AND CLIMATE

It must be admitted that black Africans can be noisy, though not necessarily for the same reasons black Americans and other poor people are noisy—except that many black Africans also live in small quarters. That seems to be where the similarity ends as to why some black Americans and Africans, and poor people are loud talkers.

The foremost reason Africans make noise is climate, and the most important reason many whites are quieter is climate-related. How can that be? Well, hot climatic conditions encourage a social life that is not hindered by weather. Hot climates usually allow people to gather in the open to socialize, and these gatherings are often noisy and festive. Important, too, is the fact that a pattern of behavior is established. When people can converse all their lives in the open without the aid of an address system, loud talking becomes a tradition or part of a culture about which climate has a lot to do. But cold climates do not allow traditional open gatherings. Can you imagine a group of sane persons talking loudly outdoor in a winter temperature several degrees below zero? Again, a pattern of behavior, which becomes part of a culture, as dictated by cold climate, is set. But whenever people living in cold regions of the world gather in big crowds, either in the open or under a roof, noise-making seems inevitable. Such noise-making by cold climatic dwellers may not, however, be as blatant as that of hot climatic dwellers simply because cold climatic inhabitants have not developed a pattern of behavior of loud talking, especially without the aid of a microphone.

To prove our point further, people who are not blacks but living in hot climates are noisy. The southeast Asians such as the Vietnamese, the Thais, the Filipinos and the Indonesians are an example. The tropical climate which prevails in this region allows for outdoor activities, such as outdoor markets. One can hardly expect people shopping or haggling in an open environment to be quiet. Even if the shoppers are quiet, the goats and chickens changing hands are another story. The Polynesians, Central and most South Americans are loud talkers.

Even hot climatic dwellers of Europe, such as the Portuguese, the Spaniards, the Maltese and Southern Italians, are noisier than other Europeans who live in a colder climate. The same is true of the United States. The Southerners, whether blacks or whites, where the climate is warm or hot, are noisier than the northerners where the climate is cold. Put simply: the colder the climate, the quieter the people; the hotter the climate, the noisier the people. Exceptions to that rule seem rare.

Technology also affects the degree to which one uses vocal power, and many hot climatic regions of the world have no telephone service or electronic address system gadgets. The use of the telephone, for example, discourages one from shouting full-throated. If climate were reversed, the completely opposite of what we have just discussed about noise might hold true.

SHOULD BLACKS BE BITTER?

It must be admitted that the memory of what blacks have gone through cannot be easily erased. Many blacks still have a long way to go before they can recover from their centuries of oppression and repression. What is more, discrimination in the United States and Britain is not lying in the casket. And millions are still under the mercy of an iron-fisted regime in South Africa. Should they, though, be bitter about all this?

Blacks, as well as others, should remember that people of any color can commit the same atrocities against each other as whites have committed, and are still committing, against blacks. If you have read ancient histories, recent histories, or kept abreast with current news, you know that what people of all skin colors are doing to each other is disquieting. Yellows, blacks, whites—all are guilty of terrible crimes against each other. Vietnamese have tortured and killed fellow Vietnamese. Whites in Northern Ireland unceremoniously bomb and gun each other down. Religious factions in Lebanon, Iran, Egypt and other parts of the world destroy the lives of others. Iranians and Iraquis slaughter each other. Idi Amin Dada was reported to have consigned about 300,000 Ugandans to an early grave before he was overthrown. Black South Africans slaughter and burn one another alive! Yellows cheat yellows. Blacks cheat blacks. Whites cheat whites. Thieves know no color. Children rob and kill their parents and vice versa.

Perhaps the Creoles can be cited as a classic example of how people of the same color can exploit each other. The Creoles were the descendants of the union of African slaves and their French masters. Yet the Creoles, too, had black slaves! It is, therefore, quite obvious that nobody can legislate love, joy, kindness, jealousy, hatred, anger, fear, or generosity into a person. They all come from within. Neither can those bad and good qualities be legislated out of you. So where do we go from here? Only one way: Be kind to all, regardless of the color of their skin. Or, better still, follow this matchless or "golden rule" of conduct: "Treat others the way you would have them treat you" (Matt. 7:12, New American Bible).

We hope we have been able to answer, perhaps to your satisfaction, the question, Did God Make Them Black? We have seen, among many other things, that really nobody was made or meant to be black, that color of skin does not affect intelligence, and, certainly, that black pigmentation is not as a result of divine damnation.

Perhaps we can bring this book to an end by quoting the statements of the 16th and 36th presidents of the United States. About racial discrimination and consequent riots in the United States, Lyndon Johnson said: "We should attack these conditions—not because we are frightened by conflict, but because we are fired by conscience."

Part of the definition of Abraham Lincoln's aspiration for America was "to lift artificial weights from all shoulders; to clear the path of laudable pursuits for all; to afford all an unfettered start and a fair chance in life."

If we let those statements touch our hearts, we will all be blessed.

Bless you.

NOTES

1. "Rage in Miami, A Warning?" *U.S. News & World Report*, June 2, 1980, p. 19.

2. Manning Marable, "Beyond the Race—Class Dilemma," *The Nation*, April 11, 1981, p. 429.

Index